Pastor to the Body of the Congregation

Pastor to the Body of the Congregation

A COMPANION GUIDE
FOR CONGREGATIONAL CLERGY

⇊

Dennis S. Ross

WIPF & STOCK · Eugene, Oregon

PASTOR TO THE BODY OF THE CONGREGATION
A Companion Gude for Congregational Clergy

Copyright © 2025 Dennis S. Ross. All rights reserved. Except for brief quotations in critical publications or reviews, no part of this book may be reproduced in any manner without prior written permission from the publisher. Write: Permissions, Wipf and Stock Publishers, 199 W. 8th Ave., Suite 3, Eugene, OR 97401.

Wipf & Stock
An Imprint of Wipf and Stock Publishers
199 W. 8th Ave., Suite 3
Eugene, OR 97401

www.wipfandstock.com

PAPERBACK ISBN: 979-8-3852-5705-8
HARDCOVER ISBN: 979-8-3852-5706-5
EBOOK ISBN: 979-8-3852-5707-2

To my wife, Debbie, our children, Joshua and Sam, Adam and Eliya, Miriam and Daniel, our grandchildren, Libi, Alma, and Yitzhar, and my mother, Sara, who together make my life complete.

Contents

Preface ix
Acknowledgments xiii
Introduction xv

SECTION 1: *Preparing for the Work*

Chapter 1: Pastor to the Body of the Congregation: Generic and Scalable Skills 3
Chapter 2: Describing a "Perfect Congregation" 7
Chapter 3: The Skills of Taking an Empowerment Approach 16

SECTION 2: *Doing the Work Through an Empowerment Approach*

Chapter 4: The Skills of Interviewing 25
Chapter 5: The Skills of Building Rapport 33
Chapter 6: The Skills of Assessment 47
Chapter 7: The Skills of Crafting a Mutual Work Plan 61
Chapter 8: The Skills of Initiation, Implementation, and Institutionalization 73

SECTION 3: *Addressing Challenges and Obstacles Through Systems Theory*

Chapter 9: The Skills of Recognizing the Emotional Field 85
Chapter 10: The Skills of Nurturing One's Non-Anxious Presence 97
Chapter 11: The Skills of Upholding Boundaries 112

Contents

Chapter 12: The Skills of Recognizing and Addressing Triangulation   129

SECTION 4: *Preparing to Leave*

Chapter 13: The Skills of Supporting Transition and Saying Goodbye   153

Afterword   161

Appendices

Appendix A: Case Studies   163
Appendix B: Sample Work Plans   174
Appendix C: The Skills of Media Interviewing   178

Bibliography and for Further Reading   183

Preface

IT DIDN'T FEEL LIKE the temple president did me a favor by saying my contract wouldn't be renewed. While I wasn't happy there, I hoped to stay a few more years, and this certainly was not the plan. In fact, I had no plan, even as I was unknowingly putting a greater plan into motion.

I immediately started networking. I called everyone I trusted and got plenty of sympathy, encouragement, and a piece of puzzling advice: "An opportunity was foisted on you," said a friend. "One that you didn't want. But I have confidence that you'll make the most of it."

"What kind of 'opportunity' was this?" I asked myself. I wanted to believe something good was in store. But with nothing in hand or in sight, how could he be so sure?

Soon after, I found work in religious advocacy as a lobbyist, media spokesperson, and community educator. I also continued working in synagogues, got interim clergy training, and spent time with ministers, rabbis, cantors, and other religious professionals. I made the "most" of that "opportunity" by becoming a better *Pastor to the Body of the Congregation*.

These experiences taught me that successful congregational clergy do two things. First, they take an Empowerment Approach to advance the congregation's mission. Second, when an Empowerment Approach is inadequate, they take a Systems Theory Approach to persevere and move ahead. This one-two combination of Empowerment and Systems provides a path to a thriving congregation and a fulfilling clergy career.

Preface

Taking an Empowerment Approach begins by Leading with Strengths—not yours—the strengths of congregants, leaders, and staff. And when that Empowerment Approach falls short, as when people disregard us or seek to undermine or undo our work, one of my interim instructors, the Reverend Vicki Hall, said, "God has special love for these people." Clergy are agents of demonstrating that love. And through a hybrid Empowerment Approach and Systems Theory Approach, we show them God's love by creating the "opportunity" to transform themselves and build their congregations into sanctuaries of hope and promise.

Such positive models appear in the Hebrew Bible's stories of Sarah and Abraham's tenacity, Miriam's bravery and enthusiasm, and Moses' rise from shepherd to leader. Each of these larger-than-life personalities was a flawed figure who grew to become more than they were. In that spirit, every person we encounter is created in the Divine Image and embodies similar spiritual potential. Nevertheless, there will be times to stop working with their strengths and turn to influencing their congregation as a system.

Had I had this book when that president told me I had to go, things might have turned out differently. Many years later I realized that he did not have a board vote behind him. Looking back, I could have said something like, "I work for the board, not you. If you are that upset with me, take me to the board. I'll do whatever they say. As for you, you're way out of line right now. So, you need to figure yourself out and decide what to do."

Who knows what would have happened if I said that? He could have stayed the course and gone to the board, and that vote could have gone up or down. He could have retracted, and whatever anger he had toward me could have grown, or he could have avoided me and gone off to annoy someone else. The important thing is that if you are in a similar position, if you feel bullied, railroaded, gaslighted or anything like that, a combined Empowerment Approach and Systems Theory Approach says there is always something that you can say or do, regardless of your situation. You always have options and the responsibility to weigh them. You may not want to exercise any of those options, but that is your decision, and the act of deciding is itself calming and focusing, which may be all that you need to figure out how to shape your destiny. All in all, things worked out well for my family and me, and they can work out just as well for you.

In writing this book, I think of Martin Buber, author of the spiritual classic *I and Thou*. Responding to a compliment, he said, "I am only someone who has seen something and who goes to a window and points."[1] I invite you to take these pages as a window into an opportunity for us to grow together in skills and spirit.

---

1. Friedman, *Encounter on the Narrow Ridge*, 438.

Acknowledgements

I WANT TO THANK those who helped this book come to be. The writing began when Rabbi Hara Person, executive director of the Central Conference of American Rabbis, envisioned a training program for rabbis entering interim service. I took that vision, with the generous support and participation of Rabbi Deborah Hirsch of the CCAR's Department of Career Services, to develop and lead that training. The training continues to grow with Rabbi Leora Kaye and Rabbi Alan Berlin at my side.

The Interim Ministry Network provided my interim training, and I am grateful to Cynthia Huheey, former IMN executive director, who invited me to serve on the IMN Board, and her successor, the Reverend Jonathan New, who welcomed me to the IMN faculty, where I continue to teach with the support of Ellen Goudy, Education and Membership Manager and Crystal Wells Program/Finance Manager.

Professor Dina J. Rosenfeld of the New York University Silver School of Social Work encouraged me to apply social work skills to congregational life all those many years ago, and I am grateful for her continuing supportive mentoring.

The staff of Planned Parenthood Empire State Acts and Family Planning Advocates of New York State provided me with two decades of opportunity and the advocacy and communications skills to make the most of it. I am deeply thankful to JoAnn M. Smith, M. Tracey Brooks, Robin Chappelle Golston, Carol Blowers, Georgana Hanson, Susan Pedo, Kelly Owens, Dianne Patterson, Fern Whyland, Emma Corbett, and Andrea Hagelgans, who

Acknowledgements

are blessed with the remarkable ability to summon integrity to advance a moral agenda through a complicated human relations and political environment.

I offer a special word of appreciation to Rafael Chaikin, director of the CCAR Press, and Dr. Malka Z. Simkovich, editor-in-chief of the Jewish Publication Society, for their generous support and direction. Rabbi Stuart Geller, Rabbi Alan Henkin, Rabbi Ellen Lewis, Rabbi Lennard Thal, Benjamin Eisenberg, and Ranta Shlobin offered valuable insights.

The team at my publisher, Wipf & Stock, was responsive, gracious, and professional at every step.

I wrote this book while serving as an intentional interim rabbi in the greater New York City area and as a trainer and facilitator for the CCAR and IMN. Those opportunities and relationships provided real-life, in-the-moment immediacy to my writing. Some of the situations and responses are mine, others were described to me, and all are disguised to protect the trust people place in their clergy.

My wife, Rabbi Deborah Zecher, has had the greatest impact on my work, my writing, and my life. From the start, she saw potential in me that I did not see in myself. She is a congregational rabbi turned artist-in-residence in synagogues, cabarets, and wherever people seek her wisdom, spiritual uplift, and voice as she travels the country and the world to sing and speak of her Jewish vision of the American Songbook. Any mention of Empowerment reflects her energy, enthusiasm, support, and counsel, as well as her trust and confidence in me.

Introduction

THIS BOOK IS A companion guide for clergy, including settled clergy seeking to reinvigorate their tenure, those entering a new congregation, interim clergy, and seminarians preparing for congregational work. It also serves as a resource for educators, executive directors, and other congregational staff.

Clergy rely on skills, learnable professional behaviors, to care for individuals, households and families, and the body of the congregation. These skills, drawn from social work, include the ability to Lead with Strengths, Uphold Boundaries, make the most of Teachable Moments, sustain a Sense of Urgency, and more. They are foundational for serving as a *Pastor to the Body of the Congregation*.

Seminaries and continuing educational programs provide a range of skills for sermon-writing and preaching, pastoral care, teaching, and more but do not show how to implement a congregational vision or manage common emotion-laden congregational conflicts or complicated situations. "Why didn't they teach us how to handle this in seminary?" we ask ourselves when caught in a board dispute or when confronted at a social hour with "Can I ask a quick question? Where was God during the Holocaust?" or "My kid can't come to Sunday school anymore this year—what can I do?" or "This church needs to move in an entirely different direction!" or "I've never felt so excluded from a synagogue as I did when you made that political statement from the pulpit!" It is as if clergy inhabit two worlds. In one, we are competent to foster spiritual development, interpret sacred texts, communicate theological

INTRODUCTION

nuance, and more. In the other, we are challenged to craft and act on a vision or respond adequately, say, when someone threatens to quit the congregation because they think someone else slighted them. This book equips clergy to respond to these challenges. It provides a range of actual practice examples so that clergy, even when upset, will be able to decide on the best approach for them in their situation and, hopefully, remain in relation with people they find challenging.

The fields of social work, communications, religious advocacy and lobbying, and, most importantly, the real-life experience of rabbis, cantors, ministers, and religious professionals serving congregations enrich this book. The foundation, drawn from social work, is a synergy of an Empowerment Approach and a Systems Theory Approach.[2] An Empowerment Approach holds the faithful responsible for determining their individual and congregational destinies, all with the support of their clergy. Instead of leading with problems, an Empowerment Approach Leads with Strengths and builds on those strengths to address those problems and advance a congregation. System Theory provides direction for overcoming obstacles to fulfilling the promise of an Empowerment Approach.

The science of human behavior, especially social work, contributes the skills of acting emphatically while upholding personal and professional boundaries, leading organizational changes, and managing systems. Specific skills include rapport-building, collaboration, setting and pursuing measurable outcomes, and applying Systems Theory to deal with problems, especially Triangulation. Social work education also models a way to present real-life situations to provide clear, concise, and immediately applicable illustrations.

Communications skills are essential. They enable clergy to make compelling arguments, stay on task and on point in the face distractions and objections, avoid negative and harmful conversations, replace blaming with solution-focused speech, and advance

---

[2]. Woods and Hollis, *Casework*, 19-20, 39. Friedman, *From Generation to Generation*; Friedman, *Failure of Nerve*.

INTRODUCTION

a positive message with individuals from the pulpit and in ongoing congregational communication. Religious advocacy and lobbying experience contribute strategies and tactics for summoning integrity to advance a moral agenda through a complicated emotional environment such as a congregation. All told, this interdisciplinary synergy of religious belief and practice, behavioral science and theory, communications and advocacy skills, illustrated with real-life, in-the-situation experiences, creates a proven and strong launching point for purposeful and fulfilling congregational work.

A JEWISH FRAMEWORK WITH MULTIFAITH APPLICATION

This book speaks to an interfaith audience from a Jewish platform. Books about clergy leadership generally rely on the experience of Christian and Unitarian ministry and invite Jewish leaders to adapt that wisdom to synagogue life, even as synagogues are of a different religion. Among the few Jewish sources, Rabbi Edwin Friedman's *Generation to Generation* and his other 20th-century writings made a groundbreaking contribution, as did Rabbi Nathan Laufer's *The Genesis of Leadership*, which built on that foundation, and these Jewish writings are reflected herein. I also draw lessons from working with clergy of many faiths in community organizing, clergy education, and in group and private clergy consultations.

Of note, Jewish clergy, including rabbis and cantors (who receive equivalent ordination), face an intensity of emotion unseen in the ministry, given the particulars of the Jewish calendar, the Jewish life cycle, and the demands of the larger Jewish world. Rabbis and cantors lead weekly Friday evening Sabbath and Saturday morning services and/or Torah study. The annual calendar brings well-attended synagogue observances, Rosh Hashanah (the Jewish New Year) and Yom Kippur (the Day of Atonement) in early fall, with preparation required in the previous summer; compared to the ministry, it would be as if Christmas and Easter came within ten days of each other. The highly popular b'nai mitzvah ceremony, the

INTRODUCTION

Jewish "coming of age" ritual, is conducted by young teens, largely in Hebrew and individually. To prepare for leading that ceremony, our children attend weekly supplemental religious education programs that offer many hours of Hebrew language instruction on top of English language sessions on Bible, Jewish holidays, history and the like. In the months approaching the b'nai mitzvah service, cantors are generally the ones to provide personalized Hebrew tutoring, followed by private rehearsals that include rabbis who typically work with the children to "write a personal "speech," that, all told, bring Jewish clergy and the synagogue deeply into individual family life, with all the rewards, challenges, and demands on time. Add this to robust Jewish organizational and communal responsibilities that include a federation, community relations council, Israel activities, and Holocaust commemoration, all under the weight of a history of persecution. Additionally, the synagogue placement process substantially differs from what we see among ministers. This book is offered with the hope that our colleagues of other faiths and denominations will benefit from considering the specifics of Jewish clergy work.

In a particular reflection of the Jewish experience, this book includes contributions from 20th-century Jewish thinker Martin Buber, known for his classic of Jewish spirituality, *I and Thou*. Buber's biblical humanism and relational perspectives encourage greater appreciation for our congregants' individuality. Buber discourages categorizing people by clinical diagnosis or labels. That is, we do not work with "difficult" people; rather, we manage challenging situations, and we label those situations and behaviors, and avoid labeling people. In Buber's language, we seek to transform I-It to I-Thou and thereby enter the Eternal Thou, where every I-Thou moment abides with God in perpetuity.

Buber's interpersonal spirituality resonates with social work concepts, especially that of the Person-in-the-Situation/Person-in-the-Environment. The "Person-in" recognizes the individual in the larger social context, in that moment, and adopts an Empowerment Approach to support mutual growth and development, as in I-Thou. As for the times that I-Thou inevitably becomes I-It,

Introduction

we rely on a Systems Theory Approach to advance what is best for a congregation, with the hope that I-It returns to I-Thou, as it so often does.

Clergy work ethically and with empathy, as in I-Thou, by upholding personal and professional boundaries, an ever more challenging responsibility in our increasingly complicated times. Older clergy recall the era of sermons written in longhand or typed, congregational newsletters distributed by land mail, all phones wired to a wall, the odor of mimeograph fluid, and a church or synagogue front door left unlocked through the day. Our congregants' families were likely less scattered and, in times of joy and need, were more likely to provide each other with emotional and spiritual support. Now clergy are confronted by increased pastoral demands that combine with an electronic revolution that calls for mastering new skills in the arts of managing livestream worship, sending email, worship, remote work, online meeting, and now, Artificial Intelligence. Clergy work demands competency in an array of media, electronic, and technical skills that, a generation ago, no one imagined would replace sitting down for an in-person conversation; Martin Buber's I-Thou is now "remote." Long-time clergy confront this new reality, and new clergy, even if they grew up with all this, must navigate the situation and prepare for additional and unimagined changes ahead.

On top of the electronically enhanced new reality, many clergy report a post-Covid uptick of interest in our congregations for the in-person opportunities we offer. Formerly unaffiliated people now turn to us for a safe, affirming, and positive sanctuary for themselves and especially for their children. One active new member said, "We are making up for lost time in Covid isolation." No surprise that more people, especially families with children, finally see value in a faith community. After all, we validate each child as a child of God, whereas schools and sports measure and rank our young by standardized test, athletic performance, and grades. The electronic revolution, scattered families, the malingering impact of Covid and hostile social, cultural, and political forces that challenge congregations and clergy also present an

INTRODUCTION

opportunity to build affirming, empowering, safe, and intimate pastoral relationships and strong and effective faith communities. We mitigate and overcome the negative spiritual impact that other institutions inflict.

The clergy calling demands patience, persistence, and the drive to provide faithful, effective, and efficient service to advance a positive agenda in this complicated era, all the while setting and upholding realistic personal and professional boundaries that protect, nurture, and strengthen us and our families. That said, there are no "quick fixes."

This book is a starting point for some clergy, a re-set for others, and I hope that you can build on what you find herein. This book has four sections. Section one, on preparing for work, invites an examination of our vision of a "Perfect Congregation" and presents an Empowerment Approach that Leads with Strengths. Section two covers the work of entering or reinvigorating a congregation. It discusses skills of interviewing, Building Rapport, Assessment, and crafting and implementing a mutual Work Plan. Section three presents guidance on addressing challenges and obstacles through Systems Theory and points to the skills of recognizing the Emotional Field, cultivating a Non-Anxious Presence, addressing Triangulation. Section four on preparing to leave discusses transition and saying goodbye to a congregation.

Section 1
PREPARING FOR THE WORK

1

Pastor to the Body of the Congregation: Generic and Scalable Skills

AMID THE EXCITEMENT OF my first board meeting at my new congregation, the agenda turned to "new business," and a leader looked at me and said, "Nothing against you personally, rabbi. But people are unhappy with the process that led to your selection."

I sure did take it "personally." Instead of a welcome, I got a complaint that stopped just short of saying, "Go away!" I was speechless.

The president, also taken by surprise, stopped the conversation and went on to the next item. The meeting ended, nothing was said about the incident, and I headed home upset and depressed. I had a contract, so no one could fire me. You can imagine that I had second thoughts about going there. But something unexpected happened the next morning.

A few leaders called me to apologize. They said they were angry and embarrassed and that they privately rebuked the other leader. They said they were committed to ensuring that their congregation is "warm and welcoming" and promised that they would not stand by silently when people behaved wrongly in their spiritual home. While that leader never said a word to me about the incident, we got along well for the rest of my time there. As for "the process that led to your selection," I never heard another word.

Years passed and I learned not to take such apologies for granted. I discovered, to my sadness, that congregational leaders commonly ignore out-of-line behavior as "not my problem." The leaders gather in the parking lot post-meeting to complain among themselves—"too bad there is nothing we can do about this"—without a word said to the one who misbehaved or was hurt. Or even worse, some leaders take such comments at a meeting as an invitation to add their own grievances to the misdirected discussion. I was lucky that time. My leaders took responsibility. They mended a breach in their synagogue's spiritual fabric as a model for serving as *Pastor to the Body of the Congregation*.

GENERIC AND SCALABLE SKILLS

> "People ask all the time, 'How do you go from a baby naming to a funeral to teach a class and then to a board meeting, all in one day? You must have some kind of superpower to leap from one set of emotions to the other so quickly and smoothly!'"

Clergy fluidly navigate the spectrum of human experience in one day, across the life cycle, from a baby-naming to a funeral, to a Hebrew school class and then to a challenging committee meeting until heading home for dinner, family time, and bed. And take a closer look at the funeral: a tragic and sudden death shocked the family and the community. As for the naming, a gravely ill grandparent almost died a few days before the ceremony. At Hebrew school, a child started crying out of the blue, and the meeting agenda included yet another unproductive rehash of "why people don't come to things." Clergy rise to serve in such moments by relying on our education, experience, and personal constitution. We stay calm and keep focus when those around us are distressed, anxious, angry, or confused. To be effective in our life cycle roles, we turn to traditional liturgy and rituals to provide support, comfort, and direction. We also rely on "skills"—an array of learned professional behaviors—to advance the people in our congregations and protect ourselves.

Social work describes such pastoral and organizational skills as "generic" and "scalable." "Generic" skills apply across a range of settings, from a prison, to a nursing home, the congregation, a hospital or the armed forces. While the situations differ, the people and emotions, along with the skills of listening, supporting, and advising, are similar. The skills are also effective across denominations and faiths. To be sure, there is a world of difference between the atmosphere that surrounds birth compared to a death, or a service that includes communion compared to a Sabbath afternoon service led by a bat mitzvah. Nevertheless, the effective pastor enters these settings and supports people the same way.

Just as the skills are appropriate and effective in a variety of settings, they are "scalable," that is, equally effective across group sizes: individual, families, small groups and larger ones, committees, boards, and the community—and when teaching a rowdy Sunday school class. After all, across situations and group sizes, people typically feel and relate in similar ways. Similar emotions are at work, and clergy respond with similar measures of thoughtfulness and heart.

The skills include the capacity to build deep, enduring, and productive relationships. They also include the ability to carefully observe body language, tone of voice, choice of words, speech patterns, and more. And, when the time comes, the skills enable us to say goodbye and take leave. To be sure, a successful rabbi, cantor, minister, priest, pastor, religious leader, or staff member possesses strong faith, expresses compassion, stands for values, demonstrates a solid work ethic, and lives with integrity, but we need more. We need to be able to apply a set of specific human relations skills across group sizes and situations.

It has been said that clergy must have some kind of "superpower" to capture joy at a wedding or comfort the bereaved at a funeral. This same superpower is equally effective at bringing peace when anger rises at a committee meeting over some routine matter. By relying on the skills of an Empowerment Approach and a

Systems Theory Approach, clergy can advance their congregation's mission, overcome obstacles to success, and achieve meaningful outcomes and personal satisfaction. We begin by considering what goes into a "Perfect Congregation."

2

Describing a "Perfect Congregation"

A PARODY ARTICLE, "THE Perfect Clergy," has been circulating for years. It describes the ideal religious leader as twenty-nine years old with thirty years' experience, who condemns sin without offending anyone, dotes on those in need yet is always available, preaches in depth but never longer than ten minutes, is very serious about the wellbeing of the world and each person in the congregation, and has a great sense of humor.

Just as the faithful dream of the perfect clergy, clergy imagine the perfect congregation, where everyone is happy and no one angers. Hard work is appreciated, and not one staff member complains about being tired, underpaid, or overworked. Financials are in the black, salaries are highly competitive, and generous annual raises are freely forthcoming. Relationships are warm and trusting, gossip is unknown, and, while everyone strives for perfection, it is understood that mistakes are inevitable, and heartfelt apologies are immediately forthcoming and warmly accepted. You get the idea, and what is more, these extreme expectations are for real.

One rabbi is concerned about rising and conflicting expectations:

> "After my first few honeymoon months, the leaders started talking up the emeritus as an outspoken, larger-than-life social justice figure in the community and

began asking the same from me, and I could not see myself doing everything they wanted. I explained that our emeritus did remarkable work, but the nature of the rabbinate has changed since he served. They did not expect him to plan programs and go to them, spend that much time with b'nai mitzvah families, teach in the religious school, be with the youth group, plus everything else. As pressure grew, I said, 'I'll leave it to you. Do you want me to be here in the building for members on Sunday mornings, or should I go out and preach in the churches. It's not 'all or nothing,' but a question of balance. Let's open an ongoing conversation of what we should do.'"

Our members and the public harbor unachievable, and incompatible expectations of their clergy and congregations. Some expect a congregation to be a real-life embodiment of Ps 23, as an embracing community alongside still waters that nourishes green spiritual pastures, overflows the cup, and restores the soul. Others seek a business-like operation that functions smoothly and efficiently thanks to committees, a board, and leaders that support, work with, and oversee staff appropriately. Fiscal responsibility rules financial operations, people donate generously and freely, all leading to a small annual surplus that, out of prudence, goes to the endowment. And yet others believe that all "organized religion" is riddled with conflict, even as they are part of it. Maybe they join us but reluctantly, as if the promise of dwelling in God's house forever looms as a threat.

Clergy, like anyone else who works, also imagine a perfect workplace. Just as a house-hunter pictures "the ideal home," a marriage-seeker looks for "the perfect spouse," or a job-seeker wants "the job," clergy often imagine serving in some imaginary, close-to-perfect community. The problem arises when an impractical ideal serves as the yardstick for measuring reality. Through this chapter, clergy can examine their congregational ideal.

That self-examination may include taking in a lifelong perspective. I think back to my childhood and family holiday celebrations, a Jewish day school, a corner synagogue, and Sunday and Hebrew school that led to teen engagement, college involvement,

Describing a "Perfect Congregation"

seminary training, and student pulpit experience. Specific events had their impact, from the way that nasty Sunday school principal treated kids to experiencing my clergy and congregation as a caring community in times of personal and family need.

You may have memories, fond or not, of summer camp, a religious conversion, or the influence of relatives and friends, even a family member, clergy themselves, who took an interest mentoring in you. Considering that ideal avoids allowing an improbable vision to become a real-life goalpost to the detriment of a congregation and career.

Under the heading of scalability and generalization, we draw from a social work model of "A Healthy Family"[1] to present a model "Perfect Congregation." Social work encourages us to consider our model of health when approached by a family in need of counsel. Similarly, when leading a congregation, we compare reality with the ideal before turning to an assessment and planning the work. This model is intended as a conversation starter that encourages self-evaluation.

ONE VISION OF A "PERFECT CONGREGATION"

Positive working relationships among leaders, clergy, and staff that:

- Exemplify realistic perceptions and expectations
- Value each person's contributions
- Respect the authority of leadership
- Encourage a non-competitive atmosphere where each success is a collective success, not a threat
- Support independent thinking and action instead of automatic deferral to long-term members, donors, or others perceived as powerful
- Value mentoring

1. Woods and Hollis, *Casework*, 422.

Pastor to the Body of the Congregation

- Assume responsibility for group behavior
- Provide and appreciate positive feedback and supportive supervision around strengths, needs, and growth, and avoid blaming, labelling, or criticizing
- Recognize and respond to change in the congregation, community, and the larger world
- Encourage respectful airing of dissenting views with the goal of reaching consensus
- Manage disagreement through Parsimony, involving as few people, little emotion, and little time as is possible and effective
- Support communication, collaboration, and consensus-building (staff meetings, private supervision and mentoring meetings, regular meetings among leadership and staff)

Support and act on inclusion by:

- Achieving decisions by consensus
- Caring for those in need, the lonely, worried, and frightened
- Affirming and welcoming diversity including secular individuals, those of other faiths, diverse races and backgrounds, and LGBTQ+ individuals, households, and families

Encourage informal relationships that demonstrate:

- Pride in membership and leadership
- Involvement beyond one's immediate social circle
- Non-possessive warmth and affection
- An openness to accept responsibility and offer and accept apologies
- Taking personal corrective action when necessary
- Discouragement of second-hand criticism

Describing a "Perfect Congregation"

Informal communication that:
- Deals directly with the issues
- Focuses on behavior and not personalities
- Rejects brutal honesty
- Upholds "confidentiality" and "transparency" as appropriate and maintains a thoughtful balance in sensitive areas such as leadership nominations and personnel

For governance and staff:
- An "organizational chart" that documents reporting structure
- Officers that each hold a committee portfolio and serve as their committee's liaison to the executive committee (VP of finances and administration, VP of worship and education, etc.)
- Membership receives timely updates around senior personnel searches
- "Head of staff" is clearly identified and functions properly
- Leaders and staff receive written job descriptions
- A code of ethics is established and upheld around matters such as conflicts of interest and proper public conduct

Proper governance processes:
- Disagreements are expected, and conflict, when it emerges, is properly addressed
- Senior leadership, committees, and auxiliaries have a succession plan
- Each leader assumes responsibility for identifying and mentoring a successor
- Addressing disagreement in a civil, if not warm, manner
- Avoids turning disagreement over policy or issues into personal conflict

- Recognition that one's ideas, initiatives, and suggestions may be rejected

Operational principles that support:

- Defined areas of authority for clergy, staff, leaders, the board, and committees
- Addressing problems promptly and clearly
- Sending matters to the board only after committee deliberation and recommendation, without rushing unfinished business to a vote
- Sending new business to committees before going to the board

Fiscal management:

- Financial decisions reflect vision, mission, and goals under an umbrella of faith values
- Board members receive proper financial information, including scheduled, timely, and written income and expense reports
- Financial records receive external review
- There are regular searches for "unclaimed property"

Communications:

- Print and social media communications are timely, clear, and attractive
- A distribution plan supports social media promotion

Now, what do we do with all this?

- Move the organization toward its goals through problem-solving
- Increase skills through capacity-building
- Establish ways of working that will endure

Describing a "Perfect Congregation"

And, as a spiritual dimension:

- Honor personal autonomy
- Demonstrate respect for communal and personal boundaries
- Summon the gumption to stand behind spoken values

PROPER GOVERNANCE STRUCTURE AND PROCESS

A Healthy Congregation operates under a proper governance structure and process. That means the board is responsible for significant decisions, and committees decide the rest. Matters come to the board through committees via an executive committee composed of senior leaders. Proposals must be reviewed by a committee and the executive committee before going to the board. The board does not consider new business, and new business is not "sprung" on the board. New business goes to committee first. While any congregation or staff member is free to take an issue to the board, the best practice would have the issue ascend the decision-making ladder. A departmental vice president oversees the progress of any proposal and, in addition to the committee chair and any responsible staff person, can discuss it at every level.

Consider a proposal to repave the temple driveway. Those responsible include the executive director, building committee chair, and—given that money is involved—a finance committee representative. For procedure, the building committee hears out the situation, weighs the options, and, with money involved in the consideration, seeks the approval of the finance committee. Next, the departmental vice president takes the proposal to the executive committee for review and recommendation. Finally, the proposal goes to the board for approval and then out to bid.

That is a lot, but such is due diligence. First, four levels of review—building, finance, executive, board—offer opportunities to flesh out the issues, such as necessity, cost, priority, and troubleshooting, all intended to spare the board the burden of taking on the committee-level work. Second, multiple levels of review inform a broad swath of leadership of the need and the plan. Thus, when a member asks a board member, "Why are we paying all that money for asphalt? The driveway was in good enough shape," leaders are in the know and can respond accurately and immediately.

Layers of repeated deliberation also allow the airing of questions before going to the board, thereby increasing the board's efficient operation and reducing the possibility of a blow up. Disagreement is more likely, and likely more pitched, when a proposal bypasses the responsible committee and heads straight to the board without review. To be sure, leaders and staff may become impatient having to hear repeatedly about asphalt. People will tell you that "in my office, someone sits down and decides without all this talking." But a congregation functions best by following a proper governance process.

Look what happened when someone took a shortcut.

> "With all the tough winter weather, the parking lot became 'one big pothole' and needed immediate repair. The executive director and the house chair rushed to get a few bids, and went right to the board, only to be sent back to make some changes to the proposal and get more bids. Had the chair or the executive director only spoken with the executive committee before going to the board, they would have been weeks ahead of where they were. They did not think that what looked like the quickest path would turn out to be the longest."

People sometimes convince themselves "this program is so great—how could anyone possibility object to it?" Rest assured, someone will. Sending new or unfinished business directly to the board is inefficient and risky.

> "The leaky roof was due for extensive repairs, and the house committee chair, who has been a committee of just one for years, took some bids, skipped over the executive committee, and went right to the board for a vote. While the proposal passed unanimously, it took almost an hour of deliberation to address the concerns and get to the vote. We would have saved plenty of people's time had there been an executive committee review."

Smaller congregations are especially challenged. Fewer leaders hold multiple positions, and even then, committees are not fully populated or functional, leaving the default to send new business directly to the board.

> "A board member went directly to the board to implement a restrictive policy. Instead of sending it back to committee, the board passed the policy. It was never enforced—everyone knew that—and by the next board meeting, the policy's proponent was furious. 'Why did we vote? Don't our votes mean anything?' It was clear that he bullied his way to approval on paper, without anyone buying into it."

DISAGREEMENT VERSUS CONFLICT AND THE IMPORTANCE OF VISION

There will be disagreement in the Healthy Congregation. People will disagree over vision, that is, over the best way to bring the mission to life, as well as over goals, which are the specific ways of making the mission and vision real. Conflict erupts when disagreement goes beyond that matter at hand to become angry and personal. Reaching a consensus vision and acting on that vision under proper governance structure is the best way to prevent and tamp down conflict and disagreement. More than just a political ploy to keep peace in the home, working toward even modest goals brings members together on a task, strengthens communal bonds, and contributes strength and vitality to a congregation.

We have now covered one model of what goes into a Healthy Congregation. This model includes a sound governance structure and a vision that advances the mission. The next section discusses how to advance a vision through an Empowerment Approach that Leads with Strengths, how to Build Rapport, and how to conduct an assessment that generates goals and a mutual work plan. There will be challenges and obstacles, and we will deal with those later. For now, we turn to an Empowerment Approach that Leads with Strengths.

3

The Skills of Taking an Empowerment Approach

As an interim entering a new congregation, someone always compares me to an external consultant who summons their experience and expertise to tell the leaders what to do. When I hear that, I say, "Not quite that. My expertise is in partnering with you as you decide what you want. *You and the board decide.* Not me."

> Rabbi Hayyim of Zans taught,
> "Let us join hands and look for the way together."[1]

Unlike a for-hire outsider brought in to give orders, clergy do well to take an Empowerment Approach. An Empowerment Approach is a leadership model that puts people in charge of their personal and communal lives so that they act to their benefit, all with the support of the clergy. Rather than having the clergy tell people how to think and decide, an Empowerment Approach calls the clergy to respect the faithful for their aspirations, honor their autonomy, and affirm that each person, regardless of their background, interests, or personality, makes a unique contribution

---

1. Buber, *Tales of the Hasidim: Later Masters*, 213.

The Skills of Taking an Empowerment Approach

to the growing good of the congregation. An Empowerment Approach "leads from behind" with advice, suggestions, support, and candid critique. Instead of "leading from the front" by pointing to one's training, experience, or commitment as a basis for deciding for others, an Empowerment Approach means partnership that empowers people to lead for themselves, even when we are convinced that they act against their best interests. As an expression of empathy, it supports them to be self-responsible.[2]

An Empowerment Approach is effective pastorally.

> "The bar mitzvah student was convinced he couldn't read Hebrew from the Torah scroll, but I was convinced he could. The parents almost begged me to let him take a shortcut by reading an English character transliteration instead of having to deal with un-vocalized Hebrew text. I said, 'Let's give him a chance at the next practice rehearsal. I bet he can do it, and I will give him the support he needs.'"

It is effective with congregational leaders.

> "After the leaders and I did our best to help the office manager avoid those angry outbursts, I urged the leaders to let her go, but they resisted. They agreed that, in their personal work, they would not tolerate such behavior. They said, 'But she knows where everything is' at the church, and they asked for more time to help her. I was convinced they were avoiding confrontation, but I believe that tenure is their decision, so I went along with them. Finally, when the bookkeeper, who we all loved, threatened to quit because of the office manager, the leaders took responsibility with my support and did the right thing."

An Empowerment Approach works with those who care about their congregation, and we know that the faithful will often fall short and render this approach ineffective or detrimental. Moreover, some people should be kept away from responsibility. These

---

2. Buber, *Tales of the Hasidim: Later Masters*, 213.

concerns are to be taken very seriously and will be discussed under Upholding Boundaries and Triangulation.

LEADING WITH STRENGTHS

"My pastoral care instructor said that when someone comes to us and says, 'I failed with family. I lost my job. I may lose my home. Everything I touch turns to garbage. I fail at everything,' we are to Lead with Strengths. Say, 'Do you know how hard it is to walk into a clergy study and open your heart to a stranger? Many people are not that strong. You are honest with yourself and realize you need help. You made an appointment, came in on time, and bared your soul to me, a stranger. You are risking being judged and blamed. Don't take this bravery and strength for granted. Only strong people do this.'"

Strengths are attributes that contribute to success[3] such as the ability to establish and pursue goals, the tenacity to stick with them, and the resilience to persist despite setbacks. A congregation's strengths are evident in accomplishments like financial stability, strong programs, and positive working partnerships among staff and leaders. Strengths also appear in humility and in the courage to admit failure and seek help. Asking for help, often mistaken for weakness, is a particularly significant strength. Asking for help takes self-confidence. It demonstrates the courage to admit imperfection, risk negative judgment, and recognize that someone else may know better than me. Leading with Strengths acknowledges failure and does not sweep over it but does not dwell on it either.

Leading with failure chases people away. Why join a church that welcomes prospective members with talk of decline? What cantor or minister seeking a congregation goes somewhere that introduces itself with complaints? What is more, pasting on labels like "damaged," "broken," "hurting," and "toxic" creates an expectation of continuing failure. It ignores what is good and

---

3. Hepworth et al., *Direct Social Work Practice*, 72–75, 194–95.

communicates that success is beyond reach. In contrast, opening a conversation with success says that a positive history can repeat itself. Leading with Strengths reframes failure as opportunities. It says, "We have a proven record of fixing things, and we can tackle this challenge, too." Replacing a label of "Failure" with one about "Achievement" charts a path to success.

Finally, Leading with Strengths reflects a congregation's mission. It makes a spiritual statement that no matter how hopeless a situation may seem, people can improve their circumstances, even incrementally, and advance themselves and their community.

THE INTERVIEW IS YOUR FIRST HOUR OF WORK

It is especially important to Lead with Strengths (their strengths, not yours!) during an interview, especially when a congregation leads with failure. The interview is your first hour of work, so take that hour to Lead with Strengths:

> "After decades of settled work, I decided to go interim, but I couldn't get hired. I got interviews, and then each lead went dead. I knew I was doing something wrong and something had to change. Then, I remembered a supervisor saying, 'Lead with strengths,' and I applied that thinking to my interviews. Instead of talking about their problems, or my success someplace else, I talked about their accomplishments and positives: a committed staff and leaders, a solid preschool, an exciting music program—and the results were miraculous. I quickly got offers and got hired."

Entering an atmosphere of failure with a reality-based supportive message turns negative feelings into positive energy. The amount of emotion is the same, but Leading with Strengths redirects the momentum in an optimistic direction that contributes to a positive view of you.

> Rabbi Pinhas of Koretz taught, "When someone wants to sing, but cannot lift their voice, and along comes another who can sing, then the one who could not lift their voice can sing, and both will sing together."[4]

Strength is in an ongoing program or activity that stands out as exceptional among congregations.

> "I went into that Zoom interview realizing that they were dealing with two painful losses: the loss of a building and the loss of a beloved minister, all at the same time. But you could see by their questions and how they listened to me that they were persevering and pushing forward. So, I told them that they should be proud of their tenacity and that their persistence was yielding remarkably positive outcomes. Many congregations don't have the capacity to do what they are doing. I didn't make anything up. I just described what I saw. They perked up. Their mood changed immediately."

Leading with Strengths turns pessimism into hope, even on Zoom.

Strengths show up on the application or in initial conversations. There is strength in a solid preschool program, well-attended adult continuing education offerings, successful teen engagement, or in devoted and determined leaders, who, throughout crises, put their reputation on the line to make things better. Even the most marginally functioning congregation does something well, be it an educational program or social events, and it is important to enter initial conversations with a positive first step.

In the very least, there is strength in a plea for help. The admission, "We don't know everything. We need support and advice" demonstrates the strength of humility and replaces problem-based talk with forward-looking conversation. Yes, we need to examine history and learn from failure and setbacks, but first we Lead with Strengths that often "hide in plain sight" until an outsider comes along and calls attention to them.

---

4. Buber, *Tales of the Hasidim: Early Masters*, 126.

The Skills of Taking an Empowerment Approach

Take an Empowerment Approach that Leads with Strengths when reinvigorating in a settled position or when interviewing. There are more interview skills to consider in the next chapter.

Section 2

Doing the Work Through an Empowerment Approach

4

The Skills of Interviewing

I saw the worry on each face, in each one of those tiny Zoom boxes. Among their concerns, they asked, "When you get here, what will you change?" That question rises out of concern that new clergy would upend everything they love and worked so hard to create. "It will take time for all of us to adjust at first," I said and added that I would rely on their feedback and take it seriously. Keeping an Empowerment Approach in mind, I added, "We are partners. I am not going to force anything on you. We will work together to make the changes you believe are right."

Beyond Leading with Strength in an interview, continue to follow an Empowerment Approach. Demonstrate respect for what they think and do. Also, show genuine curiosity about your interviewers and the congregation. Be mindful that, as much as they say they want to get to know you, they really want you to get to know them:

> "The search committee chair called to schedule a Zoom. I could tell that he wanted to talk, so I stayed on the phone. It didn't seem like much of a conversation, but it was clear that he wanted to know what a phone conversation with me would be like. I made sure to ask a couple of questions to show I was listening to him and thinking about what he was saying. He did most of the talking."

Be curious. Without looking like you are dodging a question, turn the conversation away from you and talk about them.

> "They described their relocation plan in the application and said more about it during the interview. It was a complicated plan. They asked me if I had experience with a situation like this. I responded, 'Not really. I have seen somewhat similar situations, but you are unique. There is no one I know of who is doing it exactly like this. I look forward to learning more. Can you give me a couple more details?'"

Candidates generally see interviews as an opportunity to showcase their experience and accomplishments. On the surface, a search committee says it wants that, but more than that, they want reassurance that you are excited to get to know them and understand them, who they are, and what they need. They want you to hear your enthusiasm to partner with them and move forward. In other words, each congregation is so unique that relying on your humility, drive, and curiosity will get you further than bragging about what you did or are doing for others. When asked about your experience elsewhere, say a few words and then turn the conversation to what you will do with them.

We are getting ahead of ourselves by discussing the interview before the resume.

RESUME TIPS

The resume should include an opening sentence that describes who you are and what you seek. For example:

- Minister with a decade of religious education experience seeks a full-time position as educational director.
- Cantor with pastoral care certification seeks chaplaincy position.
- Rabbi with management training and demonstrated community leadership seeks senior rabbi position.

Organize work experience by topic rather than chronologically:

- Place relevant experience first so that your interviewer does not have to hunt through the resume to find what they want.
- Go beyond a simple listing of positions and responsibilities. Be specific about your accomplishments. Do not leave it to the interviewer to figure out how you will apply those skills to this new position. For example:
    » A revised middle school curriculum increased post-b'nai mitzvah religious school retention by 30 percent.
    » A weekend study retreat and social time engaged new members.
    » Widely publicized family worship attracted prospective members who joined the congregation.
    » A congregational trip offered educational, worship, and social activities that brought members closer together as community.

PRIOR TO THE INTERVIEW

Avoid jumping to conclusions based on initial conversations with denominational officials or others. You spoke to one person with specific information and a personal perspective. No individual can give you everything you need to know.

> "The placement office said that this congregation is particularly concerned about family education, but when I raised my experience in that area a couple of times, they ignored it. I figured that the placement office got it wrong, got confused, or spoke to the few who felt that way."

Reserve judgment about negative reports:

> "Everyone said the place is so troubled that I should reconsider applying. But I had a different impression at the interview, and, despite my concerns, I accepted the

Pastor to the Body of the Congregation

invitation to go there. Those negative rumors were based on old and outdated information."

Review written materials

- Mission statement
- Website
- Application
    » What are they proud of?
    » What help are they seeking?
    » Are they looking for clergy to serve as a:
        - Partner?
        - Fixer?
        - Community leader?
        - Teacher?

Tips for Zoom

- Silence your phone, but leave it on so you can be reached in case of technical problems
- Have water nearby
- Pay attention to your camera background
- Attend to the lighting, shadows, and glare
- During the interview, look at the camera, not at the people
- Avoid darting eyes

Consider the nature of the questions

- Businesslike or relational?
    - "How will you have a strong start on 'day one?'" vs. "How can we help you have a strong start?"
    - "What makes you the best person for us?" vs. "What do you bring to the congregation?"
    - "We need someone with gravitas. How do you fit that description?" vs. "We are looking for someone to grow with us."
- Demonstrating suspicion
    - "Why are you leaving your current congregation?"
    - "How do you react when someone disagrees with you?"
    - "Why would you want to come here, given all the problems we have?"
- Personal questions
    - "What does your spouse think of us?"
    - "How will your children adjust?"

Attend to:

- Internet etiquette
    - Were some search committee members off-camera during Zoom?
    - Did they request permission to record the interview?
- Body language
- How they interact among themselves

"What can we do to help you have a strong start?"

This is an important question. Leaders may fail to realize that peripheral members of the congregation rely on them for "inside news" about the congregation. An officer runs into someone at the gym and, instead of speaking positively, rattles off their list of peeves without realizing that their negativity damages the standing of the congregation in the eyes of its members.

> "At the end of the first interview, the chair asked me, 'What can we do to help you now?' I said, 'You are the congregation's 'ambassadors.' You have current and accurate information. When a neighbor asks you about the temple, find something good to say. They will decide about membership and contributions based on what you tell them. Don't make anything up. Be positive. You can say you are looking forward to a strong interim tenure.' One of the committee members turned bright red as I spoke. I guess she heard me."

"Do you have any questions for us?"

Just about every interview ends with "do you have any questions for us?" Keep in mind that the questions we ask reveal as much as the answers we provide. Asking a closing question about their search "timetable" can be interpreted as a sign of anxiety. Besides, you probably know the answer: "as soon as possible." Asking about housing, salary, or work hours communicates that doing the job is not your priority; ask that after being offered the position. A better response to "do you have any questions for us?" is to invite a personal response—"your application offers a solid perspective on the congregation"—and then ask, "Could two or three of you tell me in your own words:

- "What do you want to see happen in the coming year or two?"
- "What does the congregation need now?"
- "What are you most proud of about the congregation?"
- "If you had one wish for the congregation, what would it be?"

These questions reflect your curiosity and build rapport.

SETTING BOUNDARIES DURING INTERVIEWS

Clergy are in a service profession and are expected to be responsive to the needs of others. It is, nevertheless, important to avoid compromising self-interests for the sake of getting an offer.

> The president said, 'You are our first choice. But we need to interview one more candidate. Would you call us if you get another offer?' I wanted to agree since they were my first choice, too. But I had to put myself first. I said, 'I wish I could help you here, but I cannot make that promise. You are also my first choice, and if you made me an offer now, I would accept it. But if something else comes in sooner, I am sure that you can understand that I may need to accept that instead.'"

This minister brought the matter to "here and now."

Sometimes leaders overshare:

> "They began the second interview by saying that they liked me a lot, but my pulpit presence is not as strong as their current minister. I said, 'Yes, ministers come with a variety of skills and have a range of appeal. Since you are interviewing me as an interim, what I do here will inform your search.'"

Other times, people say one thing at an interview, and the reality turns out to be otherwise.

> "When I met the emeritus, he said he would serve as my loyal assistant. It quickly became clear that he was anything but 'loyal.'"

Attend to questions that appear to conceal larger concerns. For instance, the question "do you wear a pulpit robe, or do you prefer a business suit?" is one question wrapped around another. Show you are listening, but ask for clarification:

Pastor to the Body of the Congregation

> "I'd consider the current pulpit practice. What are you doing now?"

And after you get the response, and if you are comfortable, you can say:

> "I will probably continue what you have been doing, at least from the outset. But I want to learn more."

Talk about what you will likely do without making a commitment.

If you are in negotiation, do not overly worry that a reasonable and calmly stated request will result in a withdrawn offer. Take their offer as a sign of an emotional commitment to you. Clergy hold their ground by saying:

> "When it came time to discuss salary, they asked me to move from my home 20 miles away to be closer to the church. I said that I wished I could but would be unable to buy a house in their community at that salary level, and the negotiations progressed smoothly from there."

One rabbi wanted to be clear about the need for an experienced musical support on the pulpit.

> "When they asked me if I needed a soloist, I told them that I could sing, but they would be happier with a formally trained voice. Things went well from there."

If you are serious about looking for work, seek as many interviews as possible. You will learn something from each one, and your interview performance will improve. Moreover, it is a good idea to seek an interview even when there is only a remote chance that you will accept the invitation to serve as their clergy. One never knows how things will work out.

So, congratulations! You accepted an invitation and are starting a new congregation! As a next step under an Empowerment Approach, you will focus on Building Rapport.

5

The Skills of Building Rapport

WALKING INTO A NEW congregation feels like walking into a theater after the movie began. Everyone else knows what happened. You are the only one that doesn't, and you are left to your own to figure out the past by watching what is going on now. Meanwhile, the story advances as you fall even further behind. Of course, there's a big difference between serving at church and watching a movie. For one, at the theater you just sit there, but at the church you play the lead, and you step into that role by Building Rapport.[1] Building Rapport is about entering relationships through conversations with individuals, households, and families.

A new priest's initial weeks fill with "meet and greets" intended to get everyone acquainted. To be sure, sitting down with a dozen people for ninety minutes is more efficient than having separate meetings, but beyond conversations about where you are from or what people do for a living, or superficial back-and-forth about the congregation, there will be little substantial discussion or Rapport-Building. A better plan involves sitting down for one-to-ones and listening carefully to what people say. Such individual or family meetings are an opportunity to demonstrate genuine concern, have a candid conversation, learn about the congregation, or, if you are settled and reenergizing, renew a relationship.

1. Hepworth et al., *Direct Social Work Practice*, 38–40.

> *In the beginning is relation.*[2]

People are more forthcoming in private and less distracted by what others say or think. They speak more freely and provide a fuller picture of themselves and the congregation. They appreciate the personal touch and will go out and spread the good word about you and the congregation. They will also come away from your time together with a positive memory that will benefit your relationship going forward. Individual conversations are a hallmark of the clergy calling. Taking the time for people demonstrates your work ethic and shows you care.

THEY ARE ASSESSING US

Building Rapport works both ways—they are assessing us while we are assessing them. What is more, just as a new clergy have a preexisting opinion of a congregation, anyone walking into your study carries presumptions about you based on superficial traits like age, gender, background, appearance, or where you went to school. Perhaps they heard something positive from a friend or saw something on the internet they did not appreciate. Maybe they had an unfavorable reaction at the interview or loved your trial sermon. Maybe they liked another candidate better. Maybe they want you to stay for life but worry that you, like your predecessor, are using their congregation as a stepping stone to a larger place. In the case of an interim, they might think that "real" clergy stay in one congregation instead of jumping from congregation to congregation like you do.

> "The president came into my office while I was unpacking, looked at all the boxes, and said, 'Man, I don't envy you, having to pick up every year.' I just smiled, shrugged, and said, 'I like it. It's exciting to meet new people and take on new challenges.'"

2. Buber, *I and Thou*, 38.

The Skills of Building Rapport

Or maybe they are excited to meet you, want to get to know you better, and hope you like them.

They may be wondering:

- Do you care about me?
- Should I let you into my life?
- How will you manage in such a large (or small) congregation?
- Will you judge me negatively for what I say?
- How carefully will you listen to me?
- Will you keep what I tell you secret?
- Will you be able to help me?
- How will you protect me when I feel threatened?
- How hard will you work?
- What do you do when people disagree with you? What do you do when people disagree with each other?
- Will you accept criticism?
- How will you react when I bring up something painful about me or my family?
- What is your hidden agenda?
- What have you heard about us? If you heard the negative things that I know, why would you come here?

If you are new, especially if you are an interim, some will see you as an "outsider," in a way that could be positive, negative, or a mix of both. Some will respect your experience and expertise and welcome your insights and contributions. Others will downgrade your perspectives because you do not know them and their congregation. An interim raises additional mistrust when viewed as exploiting their vulnerability to your advantage—thanks to them, you can put one more congregation on your resume and, when you are done with them, go to another place you do not care about either. Regardless of their expectations, you are there to do the work.

Pastor to the Body of the Congregation

FIRST STEPS

Build trust and credibility at the outset through:

- Punctuality
- Returning phone calls and emails promptly
- Meeting deadlines
- Taking initiative, foreseeing problems, and working to address them
- Looking at people in the eye when talking with them and not at a computer screen or scanning the social hall to see who else is there
- Having an open office door policy that invites people to come in and talk

Who to Meet First

Prioritize constituencies, such as:

- Senior leaders
- Senior staff
- Trustees, committee chairs
- Support staff
- Members seeking pastoral care and planning life cycle events. In a synagogue, pay special attention to b'nai mitzvah families.
- Past presidents
- Previous clergy, if appropriate
- Pastoral care needs

Meet with each staff member, including custodians, the accompanist, bookkeeper, and others. Asking to meet demonstrates trust, interest, respect, and humility. Pay careful attention, even if someone else already told you what this person is saying. Each conversation contributes a different perspective. What is more, you may have heard the same story elsewhere, but that listening will bring you respect and a relationship.

Allocate an hour, and plan to make an additional appointment if the meeting looks like it will run over, or if a pastoral matter needs more time or follow-up

Open the Conversation

- Begin by thanking them for coming in
- Briefly describe goals for the meeting that include getting acquainted, if you are new, and learning their thoughts about the congregation
- Start the conversation by asking about their family and how they came to the congregation. People appreciate the broader interest in them
- Talk as little as possible, especially as the conversation opens

Seek Their Perspectives

Follow your curiosity by asking simple open-ended questions that lead with:

Strengths

- "What works well at this congregation?"
- "What are you most proud of?"

Aspirations

- "What does the church need right now?"
- "What would you like to see happen next year at the temple?"
- "If you had one wish for the church, what would it be?"

General impressions
- "How would you rate the overall atmosphere of the congregation?"
- "How have things changed in the last couple of years?"

Go from general-to-specific
"Can you:
- tell me more?"
- give me the backstory?"
- be more specific?"
- talk about what leads you to say that?"
- give me an example?"
- elaborate?"

When you see or learn of something that strikes you as unusual, recognize that a non-verbal startle reaction or a challenging statement can undermine a relationship from the start. Hold off on passing judgment, criticizing, or blaming. Ask things like:

- "This pulpit practice is new to me. How did this begin?"

If the congregation is recovering from trauma or negative experiences, ask about coping, tenacity, and resilience:

- "What setbacks challenged the congregation in the past?"
- "How did the congregation address those challenges?"
- "Who took leadership in those difficult times?"

Replace negative language and labels with aspirational language.

- "Toxic" becomes "we can do better"
- "Mistake" becomes "let's try this"
- "We are seeking an interim because our search failed" becomes "we didn't match"

Look for strengths that present negatively:
- "It was an awful time we had, deciding to move out of that beloved building" becomes "we had the courage to make a hard decision."
- "We were adrift without a rabbi for six months" becomes "we stepped up to lead services ourselves."
- "Our preschool lost so many members that we had to close it" becomes "we found the gumption to end something beloved that stopped working. Now we are moving in a positive direction."

How you can be involved:
- "What can I do to help?"
- "What is the most important thing I can do?"

As an interim:
- "If my year here is successful, what would July 1 next year look like?"
- "What would you like to see happen this year?"

Pay attention to body language—theirs and yours
- How far apart you sit
- Whether sitting face-to-face or angled
- Facial expression
- Eye contact
- Hand gestures
- Tone of voice and volume
- Fidgeting
- Posture: upright, reclined, on edge of seat
- Placement of your hands and feet

Responding

You can:

- Repeat what you hear
- Articulate feelings, spoken and implicit
- Paraphrase thoughts
- Offer a simple apology if you misinterpret or make a mistake
- Ask follow-up questions
- Stay on point, don't jump around
- Underscore their main points

When you are asked personal questions, offer some general information, and then turn the conversation back to them or the congregation.

When you are at a loss for words, remember that you are not obligated to respond on the spot. Ask for time to think something over or to consult with others. Promise to follow up and honor that promise.

WHEN THE CONVERSATION TURNS TO YOUR PREDECESSOR

Expect congregants to talk about their previous clergy, regardless of the circumstances surrounding the departure. You will learn about the predecessors' vision, accomplishments, failures, strengths, shortcomings, and more. Some folks will be happy that your predecessors are gone, others sad, and others indifferent. Whether a departure was recent or long ago, whether that legacy contributes strength and excitement or casts a long and dark shadow, it is important to acknowledge your predecessors' lasting impact.

Regardless of the circumstances surrounding the leave taking, and especially if it was on bad terms, provide reassurance that your study is a safe place for speaking personally. When you hear complaining, try to remain impartial, express appreciation for the candor, and try to avoid passing judgment. It is very important to recognize that when they bring up your predecessor, they are also talking about their relationship with you.

Comments about a predecessor inform the assessment. Pay attention to which of your predecessors they discuss the most as an indicator of what you should consider doing. Positive memories communicate what is most valued and what they hope you will contribute.

- "He initiated teen travel and reached kids. He was there for our kids throughout."
- "She was a great preacher. People were moved by her sermons."
- "They were always there for us when we were in need. I can't tell you how many times they stood by us in those tough times."

Respond positively to compliments about a predecessor without appearing jealous or competitive, even if you feel that way. You are not obligated to live up to or exceed that standard, but you can say that you are committed to serving as best you can.

Pivot from what happened to what will be. After demonstrating that you are paying careful attention to what you hear about the past, turn the conversation to what you can do in the present and in the future, and avoid making promises you cannot fulfill.

> "I heard from many that their long-term associate rabbi drove the program and was deeply engaged with people. She left, was not replaced, the senior rabbi retired, and internal political upset followed. I sensed that many in the congregation want the same thing they had with the former associate. I told them that I thought it was a great goal and that I looked forward to working together."

Complaints about the past should also be redirected to the future.

> "The educator took our first meeting to complain plenty about the previous pastor and hoped I would 'set things right.' I promised to try, and I asked for specific suggestions for my priorities."

When the memory is positive:

> "You enjoyed your last minister and miss her. I am different than her, but it would help me know what is important for you in a minister, which will help me to meet your needs and the needs of others."

Or you can ask more generally and less personally.

> "I am excited to be here! What is everyone expecting from me?"

CONCERNS AND COMPLAINTS

Don't Rush to Repair

Take these initial meetings to learn about the congregation and individual members. Plan to tackle significant concerns later.

Be Genuine

Do not reassure prematurely or without positive evidence. Be realistic about possibilities and speak of reasonable steps forward. Avoid the temptation to suggest a "quick fix." In the early stages especially, consider conclusions tentative. Keep an open mind, and adapt your thinking when learning something new or that strikes you as out of the ordinary or unacceptable.

> "Members told me that they negotiated dues abatement with the previous rabbi. I would never do that. I don't discuss the money."

Continue Being Curious

Instead of demanding "this must change!" it is better to respond with curiosity. You may be familiar with "the Simple Child" of the narrative of "The Four Children" of the Jewish Passover Seder. The Passover Haggadah book describes the different learning styles of

Four Children: the Wise Child, the Rebellious Child, the Child Unable to Ask, and the Simple Child. Where one child asks for a detailed explanation, another behaves defiantly, and another says nothing, the Simple Child sees something that needs explaining and asks a simple, open-ended "what is this?" Ask open-ended questions and make non-judgmental statements like:

- "That's interesting. I have never seen this before."
- "When did that start to happen?"
- "This is new to me. Tell me more."

Listen to Everything

Hear out the responses fully, even ones that seem objectionable, repetitive, or irrelevant. Again, keep the questions simple, non-judgmental, and open-ended.

When the Expression of Concern Continues

Withhold initial judgment. Be curious and try to get deeper with:

- "How did this come to be?"
- "When did you first suspect there would be a problem?"
- "Can you put your finger on when you first became aware of this (or felt this way)?"
- "You liked your last minister at first, and then your opinion changed. Was there an incident that became a turning point?"

Ask about coping skills and lessons learned.

- "Given how bad you say things are, what kept them from becoming worse?"
- "What positives came out of what you all endured?"
- "The congregation emerged remarkably strong. How did you do it?"

- "I'm impressed that you all coped so well. What worked for you?"

Active listening may be more than enough. Many people are happy to come away from a conversation feeling heard out and understood.

You can also "normalize" common or universal problems without diminishing their seriousness.

- "Many people feel that way."
- "Many synagogues . . ."
- "This is pretty common."
- "My last church . . ."
- "That's what any rabbi has to face."

You know your interpretation was accepted when you hear "you mean we are not so bad off?"

Use Plain Language

Avoid clinical terms, labels, or jargon that require explanation or oversimplify complicated situations. They provide convenient summaries but fail to paint a full picture. They also establish a negative expectation for future behavior.

- Avoid using diagnostic language like "borderline personality" or "narcissist"
- Avoid common negative labels like "helicopter parent" or "snowplow parent"
- Tell yourself:

  » "I'm not dealing with a difficult person. I'm in a complicated situation."
  » "This is challenging me."
  » "He wants something I am not prepared to provide."

Remember that you want to do what you can to stay in a relationship with this person.

Dwelling on the Past

People often say that you need a deep understanding of the congregation's history to understand the present and plan for the future. While what happened is important it is best to pivot from a conversation about the past to one that focuses on the present and future.

- "I know you are concerned about the way my predecessor behaved. The congregation will be spending a good amount of time with me. What can I do for all of you?"
- "It was hard to let the cantor go. It took courage. What do you think of the music program now? Where do we go from here?"

Turn the discussion from history to vision.

COMING TO AN END

Give a five- or ten-minute warning as "our time together is coming to a close." Ask whether any issues remain to be addressed and then ask for feedback on the conversation. Do not be surprised when people get up to leave the moment you mention that your conversation will end soon.

Before you end, share general impressions. Your feedback can include your initial impressions of the congregation's strengths, especially if you are settled.

Ask one final question: "Anything else I should know?" Even if the response is "no," asking demonstrates your desire to be thorough. If your guest asks, "What can I do?" suggest taking on the role of ambassador to the members and in the larger community by speaking positively about something in the congregation.

Pastor to the Body of the Congregation

Between preparing and having the interviews—and pre-arrival and initial meetings intended to Build Rapport—you have much of what you need to know, even before turning to the deeper assessment that will contribute to a mutual work plan.

6

The Skills of Assessment

THERE WERE GRUMBLINGS AS my tenth year at the temple approached, talk of lethargy and lack of momentum. I needed to do something, and I saw an opportunity in an upcoming milestone congregational anniversary year. I invited a few leaders to a brainstorm that led to planning a year of activities that included a special service, concert, travel, and a couple other things. The idea stirred energy with committees and through much of the congregation. The murmuring died down. It was a recharge.

You already have working partnerships with leaders if you are settled. If you are new, you are Building Rapport. In both situations, the reset and the new tenure, you turn to the skills of assessment with an eye toward crafting a mutual work plan.

Go back to that imaginary "perfect" congregation for a template of goals. Another yardstick, especially for an interim, is ensuring that the basic functions, such as religious education for children, teen engagement, and a music program, are all happening as they should. Shortcomings or lapses in these areas come up in an assessment and should be considered for inclusion in the work plan.

This chapter on assessment will take a broad look at:

- Focus
- Ideology
- Authority and power
- Governance structure
- Capacity to deliver
- Impact of size on function

ASSESSMENT OF IDEOLOGY

An assessment of ideology[1] considers attitudes that define an organization's character and sense of purpose. What does the congregation emphasize? Why do people go there? What do they think they should be doing?

When it comes to a congregation, the most important aspect of ideology is the "focus." A congregation will focus on itself and its members, or look outward to the community and larger world, or, more likely, do some of both.

An inwardly focused congregation sees itself as an "extended family" where members know and support each other and activities emphasize togetherness.

> "We are a beach community and live within walking distance of the congregation. Our houses are handed down through the generations. We grew up together. Our families have known each other forever."

This small congregation feels like an extension of home.

> "I love coming here because I know everyone and everyone knows me. We support each other through thick and thin, sharing our sorrows and joys."

Sometimes an inward focus prioritizes self-assessment, characterized by conversations about "who we are," creating an

---

1. Braeger and Holloway, *Changing Human Services Organizations*, 57–61.

atmosphere that contributes to openness to programmatic and structural change.

> "We brought in a consultant to assess who we are and what we want. We pride ourselves in having a clear identity. That was especially important when we needed a new minister. We wanted a pastor who understands and reflects us."

As compared to an inward focus, an outward focus demonstrates a commitment to the larger community and humanitarian efforts. An outward focus may include social justice initiatives that serve people experiencing homelessness or hunger, climate protection, advancing gun safety policies, or world peace as a reflection of a social justice vision.

> "We have an interfaith program that includes Sikh, Muslim, Jewish, Christian, Unitarian, and other groups. We sponsor dialogues and celebrate each other's holidays. Our Thanksgiving feeding program and support of the food bank are just a couple of examples of how we help our community and those in need."

Clergy in an outwardly focused congregation are encouraged to be involved in community not-for-profits, such as libraries or hospital boards.

A larger, inwardly focused congregation will boast of a unique history, size, or a role as a denominational leader. It may hold an exclusive position in their faith.

> "We are the oldest congregation in the state's largest city and the second-oldest and largest congregation in the state. Our members go back four or five generations; some go back to the founding families many years ago. The president of the United States spoke here. The congregation is sustained by a significant endowment, and we stand out in our denomination. No one does it like we do."

Even inwardly focused synagogues turn outward when offering programs about Israel and participating in regional and national Jewish organizations.

Keep in Mind

- Commitment to any specific ideology varies in intensity and evolves over time
- There are other ideologies
- Most congregations are hybrid
- Ideologies can be explicit, unrecognized, or go unstated
- There may be inconsistency between what a congregation says and what it does

ASSESSMENT OF AUTHORITY AND POWER

An assessment includes a picture of authority and power. Authority is a person or group that is formally elected, hired, or appointed to a decide, such as a board, president, treasurer, clergy, committee chair, or committee. The authority is in charge, at least on paper. Power rests with those who make the decisions. In a Healthy Congregation, power and authority coincide. In some congregations, a "shadow leadership" holds the power and exercises authority. Power can rest in those without a formal title such as highly active volunteers, or in large donors who make decisions. Or an emeritus, office manager, or other staff member will overstep, and everyone else is expected to follow.

> "Some of the past presidents act like they own the place. They disparage sitting leaders and their decisions. They acted to block a social hall renovation."

An overreach by the unappointed commandeered the clergy:

> "Two officers acted like my religious school boss. I alerted the school committee chair, who did not want to

get involved, leaving me at the mercy of the officers. I met with them from time to time and we did get a good project out of it. But these officers were overreaching."

Yet, an emeritus or former leaders are a wonderful resource when they support the clergy and those in office.

"The past president was remarkably helpful with the problems we were having with the building. He knew the ins and outs of the church like he knew his home. He had a good eye for what could be repaired and what needed to be replaced. He took on the role as house committee chair, never overstepping. It worked very well."

When it is hard to fill an important leadership position, leaders may see their best option in someone unqualified. For instance, a nominating committee will knowingly "settle" for anyone who steps forward, even if they lack proper skills, saying, "He will grow into the job" or "they earned it."

Committees will exceed their mandate.

"The social committee assigned the youth advisor to find teens to 'volunteer' to serve the holiday dinner. The request came across as more of a demand than a request. The advisor felt put upon, having had to take a couple of requests like that in the past. No teens came forward, and the social committee members got angry and frustrated. I should have told them that it is fine to ask the teens, but they should have a backup plan."

ASSESSMENT OF GOVERNANCE STRUCTURE AND OPERATIONS

Having discussed "who" decides, we turn to "how" decisions are made. Let's say a Sunday school curriculum revision is in the works. The educator assesses the needs, researches the options, and makes a recommendation to the school committee. The school committee reviews the proposal and decides. When it comes to creating a budget and setting Sunday school teacher salaries, the school committee gets a finance committee recommendation, and an executive director, when there is one, weighs in. All this is part of the congregational budgeting process, which is reviewed by the executive committee and examined and approved by the board before going to the membership for ultimate approval.

Large projects, such as repaving the parking lot, start at the house committee which reviews the situation, secures bids in consultation with the finance committee, and makes a recommendation. All that information goes to the executive committee for review and recommendation and then to the board for approval. In sum, committees access the board through the executive committee, which reviews deliberated committee decisions and makes recommendations. Of course, members, staff, and leaders are free to raise any matter with the board, and the board chair should send "new business" to committee. But congregations work best when this multi-step protocol is followed.

It can be tedious to sit through all these levels of deliberation, say, when changing the building locks or responding to a staffer's request for more vacation time. Yet each discussion educates participants at each level and includes their unique perspectives. What is more, repeated examination adds another opportunity for troubleshooting and refinement. Multiple reviews support "buy-in" among a broader swath of leaders, give the leaders ownership of the decision, and provide them with current and correct information to spread the word and gain wider congregational understanding.

Only "finished business" goes to the board, even when people seek to short-circuit this extended process. Proposals lacking a review and recommendation—or something "sprung" on the board—should be referred to committee.

> "I couldn't believe it, but the president allowed a pushy VP to take over a meeting and demand an immediate vote on the new fence at a cost of thousands. There was only one bid and no committee recommendation. The vote passed without any conversation. It was awful to see someone commandeer a meeting like that."

An emergency is an exception. Otherwise, leadership should resist the tendency to leapfrog over due process.

The staff and leaders properly partner when making financial recommendations.

> "I was concerned because they asked the preschool director to present a budget to the board without any committee review. I could understand that, since there was no committee. The director was OK with working that way, but I was concerned that she would take the blame for anything that went wrong or found questionable."

ASSESSMENT OF CAPACITY TO DELIVER

After examining "who" decides and "how" decisions are reached, an assessment turns to "what" happens once a decision is made. When the board or a committee decides, what happens next?

- Is there follow up?
- Is anyone appointed?
- Does anyone volunteer?
- Is follow up timely?
- What is the quality of the work?
- Do people meet deadlines?
- Do people work alone, partner, or delegate?

> "The ritual committee was considering a change in service time and decided to survey the congregation. But no one offered to take the next step. I didn't say anything because I thought no time change was necessary. And, as the clergy, I don't think it is my responsibility to run a survey. Now, months later, nothing has happened. And I am happy with that. I'll see if it comes up again at the next meeting."

Bigger projects, such as bylaw revision or major stewardship campaigns, are more likely to stall and never come to pass.

"The board agreed that a capital development campaign is the ideal way to handle a proposed social hall renovation. A month passed, and there was no movement or further discussion. It was like the meeting never was."

ASSESSMENT OF SIZE AND FUNCTION

"I was an associate at a two-thousand-household congregation and now am a solo rabbi of two-hundred households. I thought things would be easier, but it turned out I am busier than ever. How could that be?"

A congregation's size determines how it functions. A smaller congregation with a smaller staff places more work on the clergy, who may be the only full-timer. A larger congregation has a larger staff where an educator hires teachers and handles day-to-day operations such as classroom problems and finding substitute teachers. In this larger congregation, clergy just make class visits, attend special events, and lead children's worship. In a smaller place, clergy are more likely to be involved in daily school operations, teach regularly, and even run the whole school, perhaps with help from a volunteer parent. And that is just the beginning.

The smaller the congregation, the more leaders are likely to be involved in administration when it comes to a decision, say, taking down a dying tree. In a larger place, the executive director takes charge of informing the house committee chair of the matter and proposes a solution before acting. Job done. In a smaller place, the house chair oversees and administers the work. Expect to have a full board conversation, where members offer opinions and suggestions, describe how they had a tree taken down on their property, offer detailed information on how they decided to remove it, who they asked to submit bids, how contractors responded, if they did, who they hired, and the quality of the job. Someone may describe how they revived a dead tree and how the congregation should do the same. That is how a small congregation works and places demands on the clergy, who sit through the detailed conversation.

The Skills of Assessment

SIZE CATEGORIES: FAMILY, PASTORAL, PROGRAM, AND CORPORATE

Congregations are often labeled by size, such as Family, Pastoral, Program, and Corporate.

In a Family-Size Congregation

- The clergy does all the preaching, leads all the Torah study, provides all the pastoral care, goes to most meetings, and represents the congregation to the larger community
- The clergy may also answer the phone, serve as receptionist, and set up the pulpit for services
- Daily operations resemble a "mom-and-pop" store, where just a few households make most of the decisions, oversee the operations, and carry them out
- Leaders:
  » Hold positions for the long term, as if forever, and there is little talk of succession plans
  » Manage multiple roles without acknowledging or recognizing conflicts of interests or nepotism
  » Feel personal ownership of the building and activities, making emotions more likely to drive decisions
  » Will often fail to distinguish policy from administration and get overinvolved in administration
  » Allow outside disagreements to negatively impact leadership conversations, making it hard to hold civil conversations or reach objective decisions
- There are so few members that a robust committee structure and a ladder for reporting or succession is absent
- Worship is simpler and less formal

- The more colorful personalities contribute an emotional intensity that skews decisions
- With almost everyone knowing everyone else, rumors spread rapidly, and it is hard to keep secrets

Situations emerge, such as:

- A leader wants to hire their daughter to serve as worship soloist rather than pay an ordained cantor.
- In a congregation where all hirings must be approved by the board, the house chair acts unilaterally to hire the office manager's son to be the custodian.
- An officer who works as a construction contractor allows one of his subcontractors to store equipment in the church garage in exchange for fixing things from time to time.
- A real estate agent believes her child was singled out by a Sunday school teacher, who is also a community lawyer, in retaliation for a house sale gone bad.
- Two lawyers in town got into a fight over the dues increase with an intensity that says something outside the temple is going on between them.
- After months of board conversation on the need for bringing younger members into leadership, a younger member joins a committee and, despite little understanding of what their peers want or how a congregation works, is heard out as a spokesperson for that generation.

Given the close community, expressions of disappointment or anger are more likely to sway decision-making than in a bigger place. Leaders will defer to the most agitated or saddened person, incentivizing emotional expression for political purposes.

> "A dying, overhanging tree was damaging the building. It had to come down. The proposal, however, upset a founding member, who argued that the long-deceased emeritus loved trees and would be heartbroken to see one removed. It came to board vote, but the vote was

closer than it would have been because, as someone said after, 'We didn't want to upset Leo, so we voted to keep the tree.'"

"When the educator's contract came up, a leader threatened to quit if the vote went for dismissal, which it did. I was proud of the board for standing up to him. The leader wrote a letter a week later announcing his resignation and that people should not bother to call him because he would never come back. Another leader called anyway and made the case that the church is bigger than any one decision. Wouldn't you know, he came back. I was proud of that, too."

Emotions can run even higher when a small place becomes even smaller due to membership loss. People see the shrinkage daily, in visible drops in worship attendance, school enrollment, and financial deficit. Multiple and repeated indications of decline contribute to emotional churning that is greater than the sum of its parts.

In a Pastoral-Size Congregation

People will not know everyone else. There are a couple of full- or part-time staff members in addition to the clergy, signs of layers of governance, and a fuller, though not complete, committee structure.

In a Program-Size Congregation

Expect even more staff, with a part-time educator or a second clergy who runs the religious education and/or teen program, an office manager, and bookkeeper. A fuller staff demands more supervision time and perhaps mentoring. The congregation is large enough that clergy may need to limit time devoted to pastoral care.

In a Corporate-Size Congregation

The Corporate-Size congregation is even larger and well-funded, with an expectation of "excellence" filling the air. Decisions and operations are conducted in a more businesslike way and are less emotion-driven. Senior clergy focus on leaders and donors and may ask an assistant or associate take care of everyone else. Staff dynamics take on a life of their own. It boasts of formal and routine worship and a strong music program.

Size and Worship

The prayers may be the same, regardless of size, but the role of clergy varies. In a Family-Size synagogue, the rabbi describes:

> "Each Friday morning, the office manager stops at the supermarket for the challah bread and leaves it in my office. That afternoon, I go into the sanctuary to put out the wine, challah bread, and candles and go back to my study to decide what to sing. To keep the challah fresh, I leave it in the plastic bag until just before the service starts. After the service, I remind myself to blow out the candles before I lock up and go home for the night."

In a Pastoral-Size:

> "A little bit before the service begins, I go into the sanctuary to set up. I make sure the custodian put the wine, challah, and candles in place. I check in with the soloist about the music. I also go into the AV closet to turn on the sound system and live stream."

In a Program-Size:

> "On Thursday, I go to Google Drive to check the cantor's service outline. I know she will be in later if I have any questions. About thirty minutes before the service starts, I go into the sanctuary to put out my papers. The cantor is rehearsing with the accompanist as usual. Everything is in place as it should be. I go to the front door and greet worshipers as they enter."

The Skills of Assessment

In a Corporate-Size:

> "Fifteen minutes before the service starts, I walk into the vestry off the sanctuary and meet the pulpit clergy for the evening. I take a quick look at the service outline and check one cue with the cantor. When it is time for the service to begin, we hear the musicians start playing, and the quartet starts to sing, which is our cue to enter the sanctuary."

AS YOU HEAD TO CREATING THE CONSENSUS WORK PLAN

Ask:

- Does the congregation focus internally or externally?
- What is their ideology?
- Who makes decisions?
- By what process are decisions reached, and is there follow-up?
- How does size impact function?

And ask these questions:

- What are the priorities for programming, education, worship, governance, and routine operations?
- Are vision, mission, and offerings in sync?
- Do specific programs, such as preschool or teen programs, serve members, or do participants come mostly from the larger community?
- Do programs such as the children's choir or an auxiliary provide the intended activities?
- Do programs such as adult learning or a music program attract an audience large enough to justify the costs and the effort?
- Should faltering programs and activities be closed or augmented?

- How do the leaders, board, committees, and staff work together?
- Does anyone on the staff or among leaders need supportive mentoring, or are the shortcomings more significant?

This chapter presented an assessment of focus, ideology, authority and power, governance structure, capacity to deliver, and the impact of size on function. Now we turn to putting that assessment to work as the foundation for crafting a mutual work plan.

7

The Skills of Crafting a Mutual Work Plan

OUT OF THE BLUE, a board member got up at a meeting and complained, "Everything here is haphazard, and there is no overarching vision. Someone gets an idea, and we jump on it. How about some foresight and organization?" Truth is, most congregations run like that, especially smaller ones. A volunteer gets interested in something, enlists others, and brings the idea to life. A larger congregation is more likely to have a plan and stick to it. Lucky for me, at that meeting I had a consensus-produced work plan on hand. I took it out, gently and warmly reminded everyone about our thoughts and planning, and gave a couple examples of how we were delivering. That ended the discussion.

Any congregation can have a work plan and stick to it. A work plan is more than just a tool for handling complaints. A work plan presents a mutual understanding of:

- Goals
- *What* needs to be done to reach the goals
- *Who* is responsible for doing the work
- *When* the work needs to be done

Pastor to the Body of the Congregation

A work plan documents:

- What committee and/or board approval is needed
- Prioritized goals
- Partialized work that comes from breaking down larger jobs into smaller and more achievable jobs
- Specific tactics
- Measurable outcomes
- How the work is to be paced
- The intention to provide real-time monitoring
- The development of effective and appropriate strategies and actions
- Plans for communicating successes

The work plan works best when it includes and reflects:

- Mission-based goals
- Positive language
- Collaboration and consensus
- Consideration of possible unanticipated consequences, positive or negative
- Awareness of the need to respond to new information and circumstances

A work plan documents mutually endorsed outcomes and benchmarks to:

- Provide written documentation to garner broad support of the working agenda and seek funding
- Document the intention to be productive
- Boost morale by contributing to a forward-looking and achievement-orientated atmosphere that feeds on itself in an upward spiral

THE SKILLS OF CRAFTING A MUTUAL WORK PLAN

- Demonstrate that staff and leaders are working collaboratively
- Protect against being overburdened or taken off task by spontaneous suggestions, however worthy they may be
- Tamp down unrealistic expectations
- Address concerns of conflicts of interests and self-service
- Serve as a yardstick for holding all mentioned parties to their commitments

A work plan can include things like:

- Worship: Special services, new Tot Shabbat (first Friday of the month for the next six months)
- Religious school: Participation in Sunday school worship, renewed family education (one Sunday monthly)
- Adult Education: Torah Study, Lunch and Learn (monthly)
- Board, staff, and leadership development: Build capacity to support decision-making in a positive atmosphere (Weekly clergy-senior leadership meetings, monthly officer meetings, staff meetings, board training, in-service training)
- Major decisions and projects such as whether to augment or close an under-enrolled preschool or conduct a capital campaign or renovation
- Personnel: Staff retention, development, termination, and hiring

Please see Appendix B for detailed sample work plans.

BUILD THE TEAM

Building a work plan begins by enlisting partners with a shared understanding of the mission and how to pursue it and a demonstrated commitment to provide the needed time, enthusiasm, and energy. These partners have a record of meeting deadlines, persisting through challenges, respectfully asserting themselves to you and to others when they think something needs to be done differently or better, and delegating tasks. They will be even-tempered, avoid complaining unless necessary, and do not take advantage of access to you as an opportunity to air ongoing personal concerns. When evaluating those who fall markedly short, consider working with others or by yourself.

Involve those impacted. Plan with people, not for them. To be described later as Overfunctioning, our more active members may presume they understand the needs of the less-involved. Such assumptions may be substantially off-base and contribute to failure. See what happened when older leaders sought to involve the younger families:

> "As the school year came to an end, and with summer approaching, the sisterhood organized a water safety event for religious school families. Not one family came! When they finally asked the families, they heard that the kids got that at camp and didn't need it from the temple. Had the planners involved the families beforehand, they would have learned that there was no interest in this program."

Compare that failure to a successful outcome that flowed from asking people what they wanted.

> "After a few months in my new congregation, I realized we were not in touch with our college students and, when I asked, I learned that we didn't even keep a list. I invited a few parents to a meeting, and I suggested that they speak to their kids to get an idea of what they would like and, even more importantly, ask their own kids. The parents reported back that their kids would love to get food in the mail that they could share with their friends. Had we not asked them, we would have planned an event that would have been a flop."

Planning with a target audience can reveal that a proposed activity is unneeded or unwanted, or, if desired, include information that is helpful to planning. More than that, involving people early on empowers them with a sense of responsibility that contributes to success.

If the goal is shutting down a program, involving those impacted may lead to difficult initial discussions that may—or may not—mitigate the long-term emotional impacts.

SECURE COMMITTEE AND/OR BOARD APPROVAL

Does a committee need to approve of the goal, or does the matter need to go before the board? Are any votes of approval necessary, or do the governing bodies merely need to be informed? The answer to these questions depends on your congregation's bylaws and prevailing practices. Consult with your senior leadership on the proper governance steps.

PRIORITIZE

Prioritizing is a process that ensures a goal is:

- Aligned with the mission. It is a "good fit." A sponsored fundraiser for a political candidate is out of place at any not-for-profit organization. Other, less egregious misalignments should be rejected.
- Achievable. It can be accomplished within the limits of available time, money, and other resources.
- A better option than inaction. There are always good reasons to do nothing or to do something else. Be able to argue that inaction will harm morale, vitality, or survival.
- Examined for ongoing impact. For instance, adding staff will increase costs and require supervision
- Evaluated for the possibility of failure. Consider the consequences of loss of money, personal standing, and morale if the plan does not advance.

- Supported on its own or with promotion. People need to want it or accept it. Does the idea sell itself, or is there a need to invest the time and energy to make the case? Are people sufficiently bothered by the targeted problem to make the effort to change?
- Examined for stirring opposition. Any proposal, even one that aligns with the congregational and denominational mission, will receive a negative reaction from somebody. Always expect it. Consider the extent of opposition and the potential impact.
- Reevaluated going forward. As new information is obtained and the plan advances, there should be an openness to make changes or, if indicated, abandon the idea.

Examples include:

- It would be simple to gather and manage college student contacts for occasional emails and in-town programs. Anticipate little opposition, good optics, and little cost beyond time.
- Initiating an adult study retreat that would take time, cost money, and may not attract a minimum number of participants.
- A kitchen renovation would require a demonstration of the need to justify the cost and bother. Would something else make better use of the time and money?
- Combining a declining Sunday school with one at another church will save money but stir outspoken opposition.

DETERMINE A POINT OF OPTIMAL REVERBERATION

Rather than yielding to the temptation to take on the biggest problem first, start at a Point of Optimal Reverberation. A goal at a Point of Optimal Reverberation has a high impact while making efficient use of time, energy, and money. In other words, "the most bang for the buck." For instance, a goal of doubling membership or relocating the congregation may be as critical as it is daunting. Taking on a badly needed bathroom and kitchen renovation will certainly be noticed and make a difference, but it costs time and money. A goal at a Point of Optimal Reverberation makes responsible use of resources while having a high probability of quick and visible success that boosts morale and drives positive energy toward more work.

A Point of Optimal Reverberation may be at:

- A teen overnight at the temple.
- A special musical program
- A newsletter redesign
- An anniversary service
- New exterior signage
- A study weekend retreat

ESTABLISH MEASURABLE OUTCOMES AND INTERIM BENCHMARKS

Measurable outcomes and interim benchmarks are verifiable accomplishments along the road of progress. For instance, we can only measure what we can quantify. We measure the work of a caring committee by counting their pastoral phone calls, but how do we calculate the spiritual impact? You get the concern. As best as we can, we benefit from working with measurable outcomes and interim benchmarks, even when they provide limited information that is, nevertheless, useful for evaluation and planning. Please see the sample worksheets in Appendix B for examples of measurable outcomes.

PARTIALIZE LARGER JOBS

Many volunteers, though reluctant to commit to large jobs or to undefined positions, are excited to take on smaller, clearer, and meaningful tasks. Partialization[1] breaks down larger responsibilities into more achievable ones that can be sensibly organized, accomplished incrementally, shared among a larger number of people, and appropriately overseen. Increasing the number of tasks and benchmarks, as well as tracking progress, increases the opportunities to broadcast accomplishments to the congregation. On the other hand, delegation can make more work than doing the job oneself.

Partialized tasks offer an opportunity to enhance morale, especially important in a negative atmosphere. In the absence of a "magic wand" that makes it all happen at once, a Partialized work plan communicates the expectation that a bigger problem, or set of problems, is within the capacity of an organization and can be addressed. Involving others in Partialization, as well as Prioritization, provides them with a say in the process and enlists them as advocates for supporting the work. Think of Partialized goals when:

- There is no adult study, so you put three programs on the year's calendar.
- There is no standing choir, so you invite three people to serve as guest soloists.
- Marking a congregation's anniversary year with several mid-year events instead of, or in addition to, one larger one
- Seeking to boost school or worship attendance by encouraging each family to invite someone new

---

1. Braeger and Holloway, *Changing Human Services Organizations*, 194-95.

ADDRESS CONFLICTS OF INTERESTS, INCLUDING APPEARANCES OF ADVANCING SELF-INTEREST

It will be a challenge to advance an initiative that appears to personally benefit anyone. An idea becomes more acceptable when the community views proponents as selfless rather than self-serving. Be honest when you stand to have something to gain.

> "When I told the committee that I supported an earlier start of service, someone blurted out, 'The minister just wants to get home early.' I replied, 'Of course starting services earlier will let me get home earlier to be with my family. But the congregation stands to benefit from the change, and that is the most important thing to consider.'"

Moving your study into a larger room will give you more space. Combining family and adult services will save you time. Admit that these changes will make your life better or easier, but underscore that your personal benefit is not the deciding factor. Serving the congregation is the goal.

ANTICIPATE THE UNANTICIPATED

Of course, no one can anticipate the unanticipated. Any change, no matter how desirable, will have unexpected negative or positive consequences. Recognize that you have not considered everything, but you will accept responsibility and address what pops up.

CHOOSE TACTICS

Tactics are skills that influence the situation, people, and behavior.[2]

- Collaborative Tactics are effective in a supportive atmosphere. They rely on open communication that shares information

---

2. Braeger and Holloway, *Changing Human Services Organizations*, 129–34.

freely. Collaborative tactics inform without trying overly hard to convince or change minds and include education, mild persuasion, and appeals to joint action.

- Campaign Tactics involve above-board though stronger methods of persuasion.
- Bargaining and Negotiation Tactics recognize and address disagreement by seeking a mutually acceptable position. They rely on understanding of the range of opinions and may involve arguing, requesting concessions, and accepting unwanted positions.
- Discourage Covert Tactics that raise ethical considerations. They include intentional omission, exaggeration, and fabrication.

PLAN TO COMMUNICATE SUCCESS

Keeping everyone informed builds confidence, enthusiasm, and momentum. Communication begins before work starts by letting everyone know that the goal is necessary, reasonable, and can be achieved. When hitting a benchmark or completion, keep people informed, but avoid the appearance of boasting by generously sharing credit for ideas, cooperation, and efforts. Underscore that more work lies ahead and invite support from those still uninvolved.

BUILD A CULTURE OF EXPERIMENTATION TO ADDRESSES OPPOSITION

Some changes, such as sale of a building, are forever. Others, such as hiring new clergy or purchasing a new prayer book, are long-term. And other changes, especially those that can be easily reversed, benefit from being called "experiments" instead of "changes" in a Culture of Experimentation.[3]

---

3. Lederman, "Creating a Culture of Experimentation in a Congregation."

The Skills of Crafting a Mutual Work Plan

Word of "change" sets people on edge. When people like things just the way they are, soften potential upset by creating a Culture of Experimentation. Renaming a proposed "change" as a "test," "pilot project," or an "opportunity to try something new" respects the status quo and admits that keeping things the same may be better or more desirable than changing them. What is more, in an atmosphere that has zero tolerance for failure, a labeled "experiment" lowers worry about a catastrophe.

Even when success seems guaranteed, calling something an "experiment":

- Sounds less threatening
- Stirs less worry by communicating an openness to refinement or abandoning the direction if it does not work
- Acknowledges that a situation is dynamic and is expected to receive ongoing evaluation and revision based on new information, developments, and progress
- Allows for failure without losing face or being blamed or punished
- Communicates that the result may not be perfect at the outset, merely just good or very good, which may meet the whole need or stand as solid first steps toward the eventual goal
- Tells those who have no tolerance for failure that success can be something less than "perfection"
- Pre-labels what could be called "failure" as a call for improvement
- Establishes a framework to address emerging challenges and unintended consequences

PREPARE FOR NEGATIVE FEEDBACK

"The worship committee voted for the change. The board endorsed it. Now I am getting an earful from members who are upset."

Pastor to the Body of the Congregation

When that expected criticism arrives, you should:

- Hear out the concern and show that you take it to heart, without necessarily agreeing or disagreeing
- Recognize that you do not have to offer an immediate rollback to smother the complaining
- Say that you welcome this feedback and are wanting to hear from others too
- Express appreciation for hearing all perspectives on the matter

You can:

- Ask for time to think about what you are hearing
- Say that you need to speak to others
- Underscore that this is an "experiment, not a permanent change" and is subject to modification or cancellation as a function of due process
- Point out that the situation is dynamic and is receiving ongoing evaluation and revision based on feedback, learning new information, and monitoring progress
- Think "I-Thou." Take feedback to heart and remember that there is always room for improvement

And you remind folks that, in a Culture of Experimentation, this is only an "experiment."

Now that we have proper governance clearance and a proposed mutual work plan in place, we turn to Initiation and Implementation.

8

The Skills of Initiation, Implementation, and Institutionalization

IMPLEMENTING A WORK PLAN requires maintaining a Sense of Urgency that drives the work, Holding to Focus in face of distractions and setbacks, and building capacity and morale by optimizing Teachable Moments. Initiation speaks to setting the plan in motion and Institutionalization speaks to ensuring it lasts.

CREATE AND SUSTAIN A SENSE OF URGENCY

When I arrived at one congregation, the library books were in an unsightly mess of boxes on the floor. When I questioned, I learned that the old shelves were thrown out when someone's friend, a carpenter, agreed to make custom shelving. That was a year earlier, and nothing happened since. Several times in my initial months, I asked, "When is the carpenter coming?" and I was told things like "we are his next project" and "we are at the top of his list," but nothing happened. When the custodian quit, I saw an opening to ask the leaders, "When you take applicants through the building, don't you want them to see an attractive library instead of this mess?" Three days later, the carpenter was there because I aroused a Sense of Urgency.[1]

A Sense of Urgency flows from a belief that the work needs to be accomplished on deadline.

An interim creates a Sense of Urgency by saying:

- "Let's get this job done for my successor."
- "We need to fix this while I'm here"
- "Let's not saddle the next rabbi with this problem"
- "If I was your next minister, I would want . . ."

And for others:

- "Can we get this done before I go on vacation?"
- "The new cantor is coming. Can we get the office painted by then?"
- "Oh my goodness! We were planning to finish this before the holidays so everyone can benefit!"

An interim will look for a sign that shows people "get it":

- "Rabbi, as long as you are here, can we . . ."
- "Reverend, before you leave, I hope we can . . ."

Clergy, accustomed to providing a calming, pastoral presence, may find it awkward to create enough stress to drive a Sense of Urgency, but that is the demand and challenge. We note that creating too much stress threatens to overwhelm and immobilize.

HOLD TO FOCUS

Holding to Focus[2] ensures that the work advances despite challenges, setbacks, distractions, or loss of interest. Much of the congregation's activity relies on volunteers of varying ability, patience,

---

1. Laufer, *Genesis of Leadership*, 204.
2. Shulman, *Skills of Helping Individuals*, 210.

and attention span. Moreover, and understandably, volunteers must give priority to family or personal needs, even at the expense of commitments to the congregation. While we cannot force someone to Hold to Focus on the work, we can hold a conversation to focus with the hope that talking about the goal will spur advancing it.

Clergy, as trained good listeners, are inclined to allow others to direct a conversation. Nevertheless, sometimes clergy need to take direction, as when trying to Hold to Focus. Rambling meetings can be a particular challenge.

> "We were considering a time change for family services and I invited several parents to a meeting to get their thoughts. As soon as the meeting opened, one parent urged a school-wide parent summit to evaluate the entire educational program. Another again asked why I don't do puppets at children's services like my predecessor. Another wanted us to reconsider the physical pulpit layout. I said that, while these questions are important, setting the start time had to take priority because we need to plan and run publicity ASAP."

A written agenda, along with a suggested amount of time for each item, may help. When the meeting goes off-track, say something like:

- "Can we get back to the question of what time Shabbat services begin?"
- "That's a good thing to consider. Let's finish that first item before we talk about this."
- "We can talk about that after resolving the earlier discussion."

"Time left" reminders also help.

- "I need to take a call in twenty minutes. Can we come to a decision about the teen travel program?"
- "We planned ten minutes for discussion of this subject, and we are now up to twenty. I want to make sure that we get to all the agenda items. Can we table this for our next meeting?"

Pastor to the Body of the Congregation
BUILD CAPACITY AT TEACHABLE MOMENTS

I was a student chaplain, visiting people I never met, not knowing what to expect each time I walked into a room. By this point, having been chewed out by a couple of patients, I felt more frightened than competent. I entered one room, and the man in the bed said, like a loving but firm parent, "Don't walk in headfirst looking like you are terrified! Walk in with your whole body and act like you belong here!" Now, that is a role reversal! A patient mentored me, a frightened student chaplain, in what we call a "Teachable Moment."

The term "Teachable Moment" comes from developmental psychologist Robert Havighurst and the field of early childhood education. A Teachable Moment describes learning that happens when the time is right for the learner. No one needs to go back to preschool here; teachable moments happen to people of all ages

> "Education worthy of the name is essentially education of character."[3]

The Teachable Moment turns a less than perfect performance into a lesson. Instead of blaming or threatening, it supports reflection, builds trust, and provides motivation for doing better next time. It replaces embarrassment and regret with learning, turns pain into growth, imparts skill, and encourages appreciation of the mentor who will be remembered along with the lesson. It retains the possibility of I-Thou instead of "I'm the boss and you are the worker," as in I-It. People learn better when they feel positive about themselves, trust their mentor, and are comfortable in their situation, as they are appreciative for the new skill or lesson learned.

Teachable Moments are workplace mentoring tools. Routine administration, such as acknowledging donations or preparing a weekly newsletter, requires a supervisor's direction and oversight. But when it comes to a lack of ability, as with the staffer

---

3. Martin Buber, in Friedman, *Encounter on the Narrow Ridge*, 247.

who consistently leads with "no!," or the volunteer who frequently misses deadlines, or the seminarian stumbling around pastoral care, these on-the-job-shortfalls benefit from on-the-job-training through Teachable Moments.

A Teachable Moment happens when a spontaneous, curious, or ambiguous circumstance pops up and a teacher jumps in to teach. For example, a bolt of lightning and rumble of thunder distract a Sunday school class. The teacher could draw the shades, quiet the class, and say, "We're not here for the weather! Back to work!" Instead, this teacher, not upended by an unexpected situation, put aside a prepared lesson for an opportunity to talk about God and awe. Something literally stirred the learner's emotions like a bolt of lightning, and the teacher opened with an unplanned yet rich conversation. A workplace supervisor enters a Teachable Moment to support a distraught employee dealing with fallout over failure. Rather than blame or punish, the supervisor asks a non-threatening, open-ended question: "How can I help you do better next time?"

You don't need anxiety to make a Teachable Moment work. Just recognize and seize the best time:

> "On the way out of the religious school service, kids piled prayer books on a cart. It was a mess, but I didn't say anything at the time. I waited until the end of the following week's service to say, 'They call us 'People of the Book,' and I explained what that meant. Then I asked the kids to respect books by placing them neatly on the cart. After that, the problem went away."

Here, a Teachable Moment imparted faith teaching and respectful behavior. Instead of lecturing or scolding, the teacher waited until the opportunity presented itself, at book return the following week, when the time was right.

Teachable Moments are spontaneous.

> "I've been wanting to open a classroom conversation about death. The right moment came when we were leaving the sanctuary after an assembly and passed a memorial board. One of the students asked, 'Why do we

> have the names of all these people?' and that opened the discussion."

The best Teachable Moment builds capacity.

> "The staffer was disorganized, behind deadlines, and got into trouble for losing track of the calendar, and—when offered supportive direction—became defensive. One day, the staffer missed a wedding deadline and said, 'Things must change. What can I do differently?' Immediately, we sat down with a spreadsheet, listed upcoming events, broke the bigger tasks into smaller bites, and set up a sequence, including deadlines."

The mistake finally caused a staffer to become open to receiving positive direction.

A Teachable Moment is an opportunity to educate about protocol.

> "A parent called our president to complain about something I said to the children. The president asked the parent to speak to me first and then, if still dissatisfied, call back."

Rather than jump to the conclusion that the clergy was wrong, the president properly directed the complaint to the clergy and provide a lesson on how things are done.

Open with questions, even if you know the answer. Instead of "leading from the front" by giving advice, a Teachable Moment "leads from behind" by asking open-ended questions that begin with "who?," "how?," or "what?"

- "A board member skipped the committee and went right to the board with new business to stir a floor fight. The president should have sent it to committee immediately but didn't. I said nothing at the meeting, but the next morning I asked my president, 'How can we make sure this doesn't happen again?'"

- "A staff member reports that they blew up on a phone call with a leader. I asked, 'What can you say differently next time?'"
- "My music director had an idea for a program, but I wasn't sure it would work. Instead of jumping to give advice, I said, 'Tell me more.'"

SOME MOMENTS ARE NOT TEACHABLE MOMENTS

Avoid a Teachable Moment when:

- Emotions, especially embarrassment, are too high and asking questions will make things worse
- The potential learner:
  - » Has been uncooperative, unwilling to self-reflect, or resents open-ended questions
  - » Is on probation or warning and you need to keep it "I-It"
  - » Is not under your supervision
  - » Made a direct request for your opinion and you want to give it
- You are in a hurry and don't want to make time for questions and answers
- It is about doing a specific task (lighting a candle during a service, singing in the choir) and it is simpler to provide information
- You prefer to give advice

ALLOWING TEACHABLE MOMENTS TO HAPPEN

Teachable Moments are typically spontaneous and unplanned, but you can allow one to happen. If you foresee a problem or failure, you can offer caution, but a better plan may be to keep quiet, allow failure, and then take the opportunity to teach.

> "I was willing to bet the program would bomb. I let it happen, and, as expected, it failed. So, we spoke about how to do better next time."

You may decide to withold comment when failure is foreseen if you are seeking someone's dismissal.

> "Our office manager should have been let go years ago. There were angry outbursts that included offensive language over small things like photocopies. There was backbiting and excessive lateness. I tried to offer supportive correction but failed. When I told the office manager that these issues were becoming serious, I foresaw the manager complaining about me behind my back, and that is just what happened. The backbiting brought the leaders to have the office manager dismissed."

Standing down and letting a Teachable Moment happen requires insight, self-confidence, and self-control.

INSTITUTIONALIZATION

Institutionalization[4] happens when a change becomes an ongoing component of congregational life. As contrasted with an innovation that is no more some short-term patch to be neglected or overturned with the arrival of new clergy or leaders, an institutionalized change is embedded and sustained over time.

Successful programs are typically easy to Institutionalize.

> "We had no confirmation class for several years. This was a great loss for the kids as well as for the congregation. So, we found a time that was convenient for a handful of them and had a class for four that led to a confirmation service. It was so successful that we had a model to build on for the following year."

---

4. Brager and Holloway, *Changing Human Services Organizations*, 227–35.

Challenging as it is to impart and sustain innovation and professional skills, sustaining a Sense of Urgency, Holding to Focus, and Teachable Moments, as reflections of an Empowerment Approach, increase the chance of Institutionalized change.

In a perfect world, this book would now conclude with Transition and Saying Goodbye. But in our world that includes challenges, roadblocks, and setbacks, an Empowerment Approach will sometimes falter and fail. So, now we turn to a Systems Theory Approach to move forward.

Section 3

*Addressing Challenges and Obstacles
Through Systems Theory*

9

The Skills of Recognizing the Emotional Field

ADVANCING A WORK PLAN requires a Systems Theory Approach[1] to overcome the inevitable challenges, obstacles, and setbacks. Anyone serving a congregation during the Covid pandemic worked in an agitated system.

> "Concern about Covid leapt from the headlines into our congregation in degrees. One family came down with it and then another, and at first, I called each one. A preschooler came down with it, and we alerted all the school families. As time went by and more members took ill, I wasn't keeping up with the pastoral calls, and I worried that people would get upset with me. It felt like emotions were spreading and growing faster than the virus. We couldn't isolate ourselves from the larger world.
>
> "I sure was upset the following Saturday morning when a bar mitzvah family, expecting over one hundred invited guests, only had a couple dozen at the service. The family stood on the pulpit and tried to keep up the smiles.

---

1. Friedman, *Generation to Generation*; Friedman, *Failure of Nerve*; Woods and Hollis, *Casework*, 39–40.

"After hearing that a neighboring synagogue preschool closed, and that the board of another synagogue was voting to close their building, our leaders called an emergency meeting to discuss our options. People were level-headed enough to hold off on a decision until we got a state health directive. We convened a congregational health committee composed of medical professionals, staff, and lawyers.

"The next day, in just a few hours, a family called to postpone a bat mitzvah, and another family cancelled a wedding reception but asked to have the ceremony on Zoom. I saw a cascade of panic when the gala committee chair consulted with the committee and cancelled the gala. Emails went out to the members, which included the social action chair who went ahead and cancelled several events. The gala chair called the florist, caterer, photographer, and band. Some of the contractors had to be paid, to the annoyance of the finance VP, who was already alarmed about the deficit, and became as additionally upset over the collapse of the gala, which was the congregation's annual fundraiser. Money is an indicator of how complicated the system can be and how out-of-control it got. The cantor, taking a cue from the gala committee, called off the annual concert, and finances took another hit. I could see how the parts of the congregation interlock. Finally, health officials set strict limits on public gatherings, and the board voted to close the building and made our job easier by basically cancelling the rest for us. We converted everything to Zoom, including worship, adult education, preschool, b'nai mitzvah, confirmation, and religious school.

"It felt like we were as united in Zoom as we were in faith. Every committee, program area, staffer, and member had to figure out the tech side of Zoom, all at the same time. Preschool, Sunday school, worship, education, social events, meetings—all went online. Office staff needed to do things to get remote computer access. We were able to put our liturgy on a computer flip-book and were challenged to coordinate sound and music and get everything to work the way we wanted.

"Some groups were disproportionally impacted and needed extra attention. Our members, especially older ones with limited tech experience, had trouble with their cameras, the internet, and computers and, in their frustration, called us for advice and took their anger out on us, even when the problem was with their equipment. They called me and left voicemails during services and Bible study: 'I can't log in on Zoom. What can I do?' They expected me to stop teaching or hold up my service to get their sound or camera to work, or maybe they thought I could do it all at once. When someone calls during a service, you'd think it was because someone died. I responded with regrets afterwards, but I could tell that they were still upset with me. I heard that they were sharing complaints during the week. This was upsetting.

"I was feeling overwhelmed by the unexpected. Who could imagine that worshipers would send me private chat messages during worship, asking, 'How are you?' while I was on camera giving my sermon. I left those for later, too. Someone was flirting with the cantor by sending her private Zoom messages during the service. We dealt with that by disabling chat, even though it meant no one could use it.

"But there was a positive side to Zoom. Zoom was a gift that enabled us to include members who moved away or were in nursing homes, but it also brought unexpected challenges. People ate in front of the screen, watched us while they were wearing just underwear, cursed at each other, and got upset when we muted them. It took weeks to adjust.

"Financial problems got even more complicated. People were out of work and closed businesses, and that added to my pastoral load and hurt the congregation's income even more, which set off yet another round of meetings to see what could be done. Parents stopped paying preschool tuition, and we started cutting the staff. We saved money on security staff because no one was in the building, and we saved on custodial, but the cuts did not make up for the shortfall. We went into the pandemic already expecting a deficit, and it only became worse.

"Funerals became an especially upsetting ordeal. We had several Covid funerals at the graveside, as were all others. The board of health limited attendance to a handful. People could not offer or receive much face-to-face sympathy. I couldn't imagine the long-term spiritual and emotional impact.

"The larger political debate also entered the congregation. A couple of outspoken members saw a political conspiracy behind the masks and closings. Lucky for me, the leaders dealt with that.

"We could have been playing dominoes, pinball, and Whac-a-Mole, all at the same time at top speed. The sudden downward spiral took a toll on my spirits and schedule. We worried about our kids and ourselves. We eventually all caught it at home and, luckily, it lifted quickly. But it was complicated, with school on Zoom and after school activities shuttered. All this until the vaccine finally came out, and things incrementally returned to close to the normal that they were.

"With the pandemic behind us, we began to see an uptick in attendance, membership, and funding. People who once saw no need for affiliation began telling us that they have a greater appreciation for what we offer. One parent said, 'Our kids and I are making up for lost social time.' They seem to need us more. They used to take us for granted. Now they appreciate us."

It will take years to absorb the impact of Covid, yet Systems Theory helps us to a better understanding of what happened. A deeper look at Systems Theory, with a focus on the Emotional Field, Emotional Contagion, the dynamics of Distancing and Pursuing, Overfunctioning and Underfunctioning, and especially Triangulation, provides a foundation for approaching systemic challenges, protecting ourselves, and helping our congregations and our members.

SYSTEMS THEORY FUNDAMENTALS

Psychiatrist Dr. Murray Bowen pioneered the application of Systems Theory to family and small groups, and Rabbi Edwin Friedman took the lead in applying those principles to congregational life. Important Systems Theory concepts include:

- The Emotional Field
- Emotional Contagion
- The Emotional Field is Dynamic
- Distancing and Pursuing
- Overfunctioning and Underfunctioning
- The Non-Anxious Presence
- Triangulation

The ability to recognize, understand, and manage the congregation as a "system" is essential for working as congregational clergy.

Systems are fundamental to existence. A system is composed of distinct objects that influence each other. System parts interact and dovetail in a larger structure of interdependent components that rely on one another, even as no single force is in charge. An equilibrium happens and sustains itself until something in the system changes.

For example, a solar system is a balanced organization of a sun, orbiting planets and moons held together by gravity. Were the Moon and Mars to suddenly change places, for instance, the entire system would feel the impact, and a new equilibrium would be the outcome. The sun is at the center, but it is not in control. The presence or absence of any planetary object influences the behavior of all the others.

The world economic system is a network of activities within and between nations. Within a nation, interest rates, cost of living, unemployment rates, manufacturing production, and more fluctuate in response to national and world events. Famine, tariffs, or war, for instance, impact one country with international consequences. The United States and China, the world's two largest economies, exert considerable influence but are not in control.

The human body is one larger system composed of subsystems—digestive, nervous, reproductive, muscular, and the like. A change in one subsystem impacts others in a potential cascade of changes that influence multiple parts of the body, which finds a new way to sustain itself or stops functioning.

In this line of thought, a congregation is a system ruled by emotions that come together in an array known as an Emotional Field.

THE CONGREGATION IS AN EMOTIONAL FIELD

To say that a congregation is an Emotional Field means that a congregation is a system driven by emotions. It is a network of mutually influencing individuals and subgroups. Emotions swirl through a congregation and impact members, who go on to influence others and be influenced in return in perpetual reciprocity of a stable equilibrium. In a body that is greater than the sum of its parts, as we witnessed during Covid, this larger-than-life congregational system of emotions makes for more than enough work for the religious leader.

Emotions are a congregation's raw material and product. It is as if only emotions count and the facts do not matter. To be sure, we deal with facts when it comes to the number of members, money in the bank, the age of the building, its square footage and seating, yet, when it comes to Systems Theory, the emotional reactions to these things become more important than the physical reality. How a person feels about an event is more significant than what really happened.

> "As I was saying goodbye to my congregation, people told me what they remembered from my sermons, but I could swear I never said exactly that, so they were not

communicating fact. They were telling me how they felt when they heard me speak. What I said made no difference."

EMOTIONAL CONTAGION

Emotions are contagious. We act and speak in ways that bring others to feel the same way we do. For instance, a sad eulogy conveys sadness to the congregation. During Covid, a call from a distraught gala committee chair passed the same upset to the ritual committee chair. Clergy also take on the emotions of others.

> "A distressed parent of a Sunday school student confronted the educator after the school suspended her child for threatening to harm another student. The educator, who was still in school working toward an education degree, was deeply upset, especially because the parent accused her of 'being a disgrace to the field of education.' I told the educator, 'Relax. Don't take this to heart. You are not yet done with education school, so you are not yet a full educator. So, at the most, the parent is only partially correct.' The educator looked puzzled. I continued, 'Why are you letting her make you as upset as she feels?'"

AN EMOTIONAL FIELD IS DYNAMIC

An Emotional Field undergoes constant change as members come and go and their involvement waxes and wanes. The Emotional Field shifts when a new person steps up to lead, when a boiler needs replacement, or a pandemic spreads among the members of the congregation. An unexpected resignation of a senior leader or clergy will have a visible impact, even on those who rarely participate. (To be sure, those who do not participate already exert influence through their absence). Pockets of a congregation that are removed from the regular doings of the larger body will not take notice until they call for a wedding when they finally learn that the minister left. Even small numbers of people can have a disproportionately large emotional impact, as when a couple of consistently disaffected members organize to oppose a proposed building renovation, and the most competent clergy will forget about their human relation skills, lash out in anger, and create an enduring social rift.

> Rabbi Abraham Yaakov of Sadagora taught,
> "What we say here is heard there."[2]

The Emotional Field will often operate out of sight. Here a minister is caught off guard:

> "I heard about a minister who went home distraught because a meeting unexpectedly blew up instead of going as expected. The minister sat down to dinner behind a plate of sauce-covered spaghetti and one big meatball sitting on top. With little appetite, the minister picked up a fork and played with a spaghetti strand on one side of the plate and noticed a strand moving on the other side of the plate, while the exact connection was hidden by the sauce. The minister thought, 'The strands are the Emotional Field working out of sight, as if covered with sauce. And I am the meatball sitting on top of the whole thing.'"

DISTANCING AND PURSUING

Distancing occurs when one person withdraws emotionally from a second, and the second Pursues the first seeking their acceptance, approval, or a simple conversation. Instead of reconciling with the Pursuer, the Distancer grows even more emotionally remote, causing the Pursuer to grow increasingly more anxious and pursue more vigorously, in a reciprocal upward emotional spiral. It takes two to Distance and Pursue. In the Covid example, the clergy was

---

2. Buber, *Tales of the Hasidim: Later Masters*, 70.

feeling overwhelmed by the pastoral demands and Distanced from congregants by reducing outreach to the ill.

> "A potential donor, with the capacity for a major gift, was stringing us along with vague promises but no firm commitment. I kept thinking I could find their sweet spot and kept trying harder. We had dinner with spouses. I sent them a note of congratulations on the birth of a grandchild. I visited them at the hospital—and more. But the more I tried, the more distant they got."

Distancing appears in cold or brusque communication, delayed responses to email or phone messages, or when rejecting whatever is said by the Pursuer.

Distancing and Pursuing occur in congregations when:

- A donor or leader withholds approval of something the clergy proposes, and the clergy persists in seeking that approval
- A leader always seems to find fault with the clergy, while the clergy, nevertheless, continues to fish for a compliment
- A staffer suddenly behaves coldly, refuses to give an explanation, and another staffer tries too hard to find out why
- A congregant turns to clergy with continuing pastoral needs, and the clergy offers a cold shoulder

Clergy

- Pursue when:
  - » A potential donor gives you a brush off and you persistently try to find out why
  - » Seeking an officer's favor
- Distance when:
  - » Avoiding necessary confrontation
  - » Feeling guilty for disappointing someone
  - » Feeling overwhelmed by those who want more time than the clergy is prepared to give

Pastor to the Body of the Congregation

Overfunctioning and Underfunctioning

One person Overfunctions while the second Underfunctions. Underfunctioning is passive, indifferent behavior. Overfunctioning is "the helping hand that strikes again." Overfunctioning and Underfunctioning have nothing to do with intelligence but everything to do with reciprocal behavior.

Overfunctioning happens when a person:

- Does for others what they do not want for themselves.
- Speaks for others without consulting with them
- Directs someone not to do something because it might turn out to be a failure, thereby protecting them from making mistakes
- Presumes someone else's wishes or needs without asking them
- Does not prioritize and everything becomes important and urgent
- Gives unneeded, unnecessary, or unsolicited advice or instructions, especially when something is already known or obvious
- Goes above and beyond what could possibly be needed when very little or nothing is needed
- Does everything themselves and refuses to delegate because they think they can do it faster or better
- Repeats unsuccessful behavior despite the continuing lack of success
- Takes on an issue but gets distracted, resulting in a lack of follow-up
- Turns a discussion to other topics before the previous item is fully addressed
- Talks without paying attention to time

- Takes on too much when others fail to act and then complains about all the work
- Is highly judgmental of themselves and others
- Talks without listening or listens only long enough to find something to disagree over

Overfunctioning can come from perfectionism that says even minor failure is unacceptable. It is risk-averse and sticks with what is familiar, whether it works or not.

Overfunctioning appears in the congregation when people:

- Seek information that is confidential or has no bearing on them
- Plan programs without consulting those impacted
- Act as though they have unique abilities, are one-of-a-kind volunteers, and are irreplaceable
- As former leaders, overstep by imposing themselves on sitting leaders
- Provide information that will not change the outcome
- Repeat information that is already well known
- Persist in demanding things, even after continually being told, "No!"
- Jump from issue to issue to issue instead of focusing on the matter at hand
- Fail to keep focus in a personal conversation or hold to an agenda when running a meeting. They start with one issue and go to another without fully addressing the first, which remains unresolved.
- Talk extensively and agree on action, but no one volunteers or is appointed to follow up
- Get caught up in a discussion, unaware of passing time
- Turn a committee discussion from policy to detailed administration

- Run a meeting by delving into detail as a way of avoiding a big issue
- Become the mouthpiece for someone else who is upset
- Chair a committee or hold an office "forever"

Overfunctioning is present when people say:

- "We organized an event for the younger temple families, and no one came."
- "How can I delegate to someone who doesn't do it right?"
- "I can't find committee members to help me do the work."
- "It's easier to do this by myself."
- "Others just don't understand."
- "Everyone needs to be at peace with the decision."
- "I can't find anyone to take over the committee."
- "I have been doing this job for a long time, and I enjoy it."

Underfunctioning

Underfunctioning is marked by passivity and indifference. It may present itself as uncaring, or it will rise from a feeling that nothing will change or make a difference. Some people will happily Underfunction and welcome someone to Overfunction on their behalf. Overfunctioning and Underfunctioning come as a paired set and can be win-win for both.

Underfunctioning describes some who are marginal in congregational life. They will show up and participate from time to time, but, for the most part, gladly sit on the sidelines while others Overfunction and take on the responsibility.

Challenging as it is to address Distancing and Pursuing, and Overfunctioning and Underfunctioning, these behavior patterns can be approached, as we will discuss, by upholding Boundaries and responding to Triangulation as a Non-Anxious Presence.

10

The Skill of Nurturing One's Non-Anxious Presence

SYSTEMS THEORY CONSIDERS THE Non-Anxious Presence (NAP) as the ideal clergy persona. NAP enters an emotionally charged situation and puts their emotions aside to behave rationally and productively. While no one is entirely anxiety-free, NAP thinks before acting and acts rationally even in moments of great upset. Consider the anxiety before a wedding or a funeral. While the situations are tremendously different, the emotions are equally strong and respond equally well to NAP. On a congregational level, in the Covid example of the previous chapter, the board put anxiety on hold to wait for a Department of Health order before voting to close the building.

The situations in the previous chapter and in the next chapter are all I-It. NAP enters a situation with the goal of seeking I-Thou, even though it may be impossible to achieve in that moment. NAP recognizes that each congregant, even those who challenge us, is a child of God. At the same time, we do ourselves and others a disservice by walking away from a conversation having compromised a deeply held principle or personal boundaries. We are called to stand for who we are and what we believe, and NAP is our best option.

NAP is easily misunderstood. The unaccustomed ear assumed that "non-anxious" means uncaring and that "presence" means just showing up. Truth is, NAP cares very deeply and "Presence" means full spiritual engagement. For instance, in the Hebrew Bible, when God called Abraham (Gen 22:1) and again, when God called Moses (Exod 3:4), both leaders responded with the Hebrew word *hineini*, meaning "I am present." *Hineini* conveys "I am 100% all in."

Nurturing NAP begins by recognizing that anxiety is normal. Everyone gets anxious, and there is nothing wrong when that anxiety does not drive behavior. What is more, becoming anxious about being anxious adds a second problem to the first. That is, the first problem is the anxiety over a situation. The second problem is the anxiety about the anxiety that says, "There's something wrong with me because I'm upset about this." It is fine to feel anxious if you do not act that way in your professional role.

The Hebrew Bible also presents anxiety as normal and manageable. Cain reacted with deep distress to God's rejection of that sacrifice, prompting God to offer reassurance. God affirmed that an empowered Cain could take charge of himself and do better. God said, "Certainly, if you do well, there will be uplift. But if you do not do well, sin waits at the door. It seeks you, but you can rule over it" (Gen 4:7). In the same way, when passions flare, God graces us with the capacity to overcome instinct and anxiety.

> Rabbi Uri of Strelisk in the name of Rabbi Shlomo of Karlin taught, "Now, there are people within whom the good traits of Cain's soul have their habitations, and these are very great."[1]

One may feel challenged to act as NAP because one is:

- Unsure what to do and needs time to decide or seek a mentoring consult

---

1. Buber, *Tales of the Hasidim: Early Masters*, 279.

- Convinced, not just hopeful, that a problem will go away by itself (when the staffer in question retires, when a particular board member is about to step down from leadership)
- Waiting for a problem to get worse so that you can make a more compelling argument that is more likely to enlist the support of others
- Angry, and acting in anger will hurt more than help

Addressing anxiety begins by considering potential responses. Moreover, weighing options distracts the spirit, tamps down the upset, and builds NAP. Deliberation builds confidence by saying to oneself, "I am not stuck. I have choices. I will figure something out and get through this situation." Weighing choices raises self-confidence and builds hope.

CONSIDER SOME GENERAL SUGGESTIONS

Face-to-Face Conversation is Generally Best

Avoid dealing with controversial matters in email.

> "A member with a history of expressing strong political opinions forwarded a newspaper editorial, writing nothing more than an ask, 'What do you think?' I thought he was trying to provoke me in writing. I replied, 'I have mixed reactions" and offered to have a conversation the following week. An email exchange would have easily taken an hour of my time and could have been forwarded to others. I would only have a genuine conversation, in person."

On the other hand, when a matter has the potential to go to the board or involve a code of ethics, it may be wise to put as much as possible in writing.

Begin by Listening

An Empowerment Approach actively respects what people think. As when Building Rapport, listen carefully and fully before speaking. You can say or ask:

- "Please start from the beginning."
- "What do I need to know?"
- "Tell me what is going on."

Making sure you get a full picture, even when you heard this all before. Listening makes time to think about a response.

Sometimes people are satisfied to be merely heard. You do not need to say or do anything. If you hear, "I know there is nothing you can do about this, but I appreciate your taking the time to listen to me," you can simply say, "Thank you. Please feel free to reach out again in the future."

Pivot from Anger to Sadness

One of my mentors, the Reverend Tom Davis, said, "There is no merit in saying you are angry. Everyone gets angry. Express your anger with sadness."

"I am angry" becomes:

- "I am sorry that happened."
- "That turn of events saddens me."
- "I wish this wasn't happening"
- "I'm disappointed over your frustration."
- "I wish you could feel happier with the church."

Listen Carefully

Summarize the problem without taking a position. Show that you are listing by describing what you hear without attacking, accusing, diagnosing, or labeling. Demonstrate that you care about the person and the issue. Acknowledge that you understand without agreeing.

- "You say that your child had a bad experience with that teacher."
- "You sure were bothered by that sermon."
- "That was an upsetting experience."
- "I understand why this is a struggle."
- "I respect that you feel strongly about the matter."
- "I hear what you are saying"
- "It is good you are telling me this."
- "I don't blame you for feeling that way."
- "Yes, I expect you to be upset."

Avoid Giving Advice Prematurely

Resist the temptation to jump to take sides or make premature suggestions without all the information. Get them to continue talking. Before suggesting ways to deal with a situation, first summarize the dilemma to make sure you understand it. You can then say something like:

- "You want one thing but find yourself stuck with another."
- "You are 'here' but you want to be 'there.'"

Make or Ask for Time to Think

Even if you think there is a quick fix, tamp down the desire to resolve this ASAP.

- "I have to give it some more thought so I can offer a considered opinion"
- "Thanks for raising this. I need to think about it"

- "I'll keep it in mind as I weigh a next step."
- "Let me ask you a few more questions while I think about what to say."

If You Feel Pressured to Offer an Opinion, Hold Your Ground While Ascending a Scale

Responding with Parsimony, which will be discussed, reflects an Empowerment Approach and protects against being Triangulated.

- "You feel strongly."
- "This is a problem."
- "This is a big problem!"
- "This is a really big problem!!"
- "Wow, this sure is a problem!!!"

Express confidence in their ability to successfully address the issue. An Empowerment Approach suggests saying:

- "You will figure out how to handle this problem."
- "You can address this issue."

In a more assertive approach, turn the problem back to them:

- "It is fine for you to email the teacher and ask for more classroom art projects."
- "One call from you to the office will fix the problem."
- "I know that the committee chair will be happy to hear from you."

Deflate a Tense Atmosphere

Lower the emotion in the conversation by demonstrating respect and understanding. Use non-judgmental/non-confrontational language.

- "I don't blame you."
- "I see where you come from."
- "Even when we disagree, we have to remind ourselves that we are here to do sacred work."

Deflate emotions by normalizing the problem. Sometimes people calm down when they hear that others face the same challenge and, as serious as the matter may be, are able to live with it.

- "I know they are upset. The reality is every temple has this."
- "This is a common concern in our congregations."
- "Other congregations, even ones of other religions, have this problem."

You might even get a response of "Oh, really! I didn't know that" rather than be the object of additional challenges.

Be honest when you do not know You do not have to be an expert in all things, nor do you have to provide "off-the-cuff" answers. Say:

- "I don't know."
- "I'm not sure."
- "Let me think about it."
- "I need to talk to more people to give you a proper response."

Apologize when you are wrong. Do it as soon as possible, without showing anxiety by looking rushed. Speak genuinely and concisely, without appearing frightened, angry or groveling. Avoid making excuses or explaining unless asked or necessary. Honesty and lack of defensiveness speaks well of you and models responses for others. Say and, if necessary, instead of going deeper, just repeat:

- "I made a mistake."
- "I will act differently going forward."
- "I was wrong."
- "I apologize."

Pastor to the Body of the Congregation

You probably do not have to say anything else.
  Depersonalize contrary responses. Replace:

- "When you said…" with "When it was said."
- "You are wrong" with "Opinions differ."

When you disagree with something said at a committee meeting, wait for a few more speakers to talk before speaking to avoid the appearance of attacking that person who spoke.

THE SKILL OF ACTING WITH PARSIMONY

Acting with Parsimony[2] is about addressing a situation with as few words, as little emotion, and involving as few people as possible. Responding with Parsimony replaces comprehensive, point-by-point declarations with brief, non-attacking statements. For instance, rather than raise a matter with a clergy colleague by saying, "Your behavior violates your code of ethics, and let me tell you why!" save that accusation for later, and only if you really need to use it. Start by asking, "Can I ask you to do that differently going forward?" More moderate behavior may expedite reaching a resolution and increase the probability that the relationship will survive.

Keeping it as simple as possible conserves time and energy. A few carefully chosen words may address the need for the moment, or altogether, and contribute to a positive outcome. Consider the range of potential responses and turn to the simplest. Avoid responses that are minimal and likely ineffective. Talking too much or getting worked up will raise suspicion of a hidden, self-advancing agenda, or a vendetta, and turn the conversation away from the problem on to you and your emotions.

Acting with Parsimony is especially effective when confronted by several people with the same grievance. Break down the group into individuals and hold private meetings. Use the skills of Rapport Building to build or rebuild trust and a relationship. This

---

2. Brager and Holloway, *Changing Human Services Organizations*, 141.

is a better way to work than meeting an entire group at once. If they refuse to come in and see you, build your leverage by making sure that others know that they declined your invitation.

When you meet, define your position clearly, simply. Display no sign of fear or worry. When formulating your response:

- Speak with "I" statements
- Avoid passing judgment
- Don't blast out all your points in an opening salvo
- Say no more than the minimum; repeat if necessary
- Stay on that clear, simple statement, and avoid going deeper
- Pause after speaking to allow them to consider your point
- Don't attack when you can describe

Use language like:

- "I see we disagree."
- "I am sorry we do not see eye-to-eye."
- "I wish we were on the same side of the issue."
- "I hear what you are saying, but I look at it differently."
- "I hear what you are saying, and I am glad you recognize that we continue to disagree."
- "You are free to go to the board, but I want you to know that you are doing so without my support."

Parsimony also means holding on to your own problems and involving others only as necessary. If you need to escalate, involve the fewest people and at the lowest level as possible. If the matter relates to the school, for example, first go to the teacher, then to the principal, and only then to the school director.

> "As with my predecessor, the cantor did not follow my instructions when preparing the b'nai mitzvah. Unlike my predecessor who dumped this problem on the leaders, I told the leaders that I would take care of it myself, but I made sure they knew what is happening."

Escalate with Parsimony

If the simplest response is inadequate and emotions rise, you can also escalate in emotion, but express no more emotion than the person you are talking to. As you ramp up, be mindful that your behavior can be brought to the attention of others, including the board.

Sometimes, a stronger, nevertheless gentle "no!" is enough.

> "I wish I could be at the community gathering, but I have a commitment Sunday afternoon. But I can send someone in my place."

Complaints about preaching are common. You can acknowledge the concern without attacking or showing defensiveness.

> "A few days after a sermon, a board member called to complain that they felt that the position I took in that sermon excluded them from the congregation. I said that I was sorry for their upset, I wish I could satisfy all the differing positions in the congregation, but that is not possible. I often find myself disagreeing with things guest speakers here say and with our members. I even disagree with my own family. The congregation and our mission are much larger than what any clergy say. We are a community with many different ideas on the issues, and I appreciate hearing from our members as I do hear from you."

Here the clergy acknowledged the concern while trying to reduce the upset.

Parse out the conversation. Sometimes people discuss two matters in one statement. Point out that "There are really two issues here . . .

- "One belongs to the education committee and the other to the worship committee."
- "One is how we promote the program. The other is when we offer it."

- "One is over the wedding policy. The other is about what the couple wants."
- "One has to do with how the educator explained himself. The other has to do with him responding by email rather than a phone call."

Commit to an active response. Offering to do something communicates that you care.

- "I'll call that person."
- "I certainly will get back to you."
- "I will ask one of the leaders to follow up."
- "This is a board matter. I will ask the president to put it on the agenda."
- "The office takes care of scheduling my weddings. I will have them get back to you."

Make a counteroffer.

- "I'm happy to do that if . . ."
- "Let's meet in the middle . . ."

Say "no" by saying "yes." A positive voice is more persuasive. Find and highlight agreement.

- "What you said is precisely what I am concerned about. I just look at it differently."
- "We agree that there seems to be some confusion"
- "Let's begin by looking at where we agree"

Offer a non-judgmental statement on the situation that leads with "I" instead of "you." "You" statements sound like an attack.

- "I am feeling caught in the middle."
- "I am new to all this."
- "Some say this is a good idea. On the other hand, people, including me, think otherwise."

Respond to repetition by repeating yourself and being honest about it.

- "As I said, I think that there is no need to change the worship time."
- "Again, we need to raise this point with the executive director."
- "I know I just said it, but this is where I stand."

Respond with a question.

- "So?"
- "What do you suggest being done about this?"
- "What do you think is really going on?"

Seek collaboration.

- "How do we move forward?"
- "Where do we go from here?"
- "Where do we begin working together on this?"

Make it clear that you cannot do more than you are doing.

- "I am sorry that I am unable to address your need."
- "I cannot give you what you are asking for, and I respect that you are frustrated."
- "You are asking me to do something that I cannot provide."

Leave the door open to more conversation.

- "That's my thinking right now. Maybe things will change going forward."
- "Let me know if you have any other ideas. We certainly can talk again."

When a matter deals with policy or a larger issue, use your communication resources to broadcast your message.

- Bulletin articles

The Skill of Nurturing One's Non-Anxious Presence

- During a sermon
- Add a positive word after the president's speech or officer's announcement
- At the opening of staff, committee, or board meetings

When dealing with "What if . . .?" hypothetical questions.

- There is no obligation to give definitive answers to hypothetical questions
- An imaginary scenario gets an imaginary response

IN SUM, DO NOT:

- Attack
- Overexplain by providing unnecessary details or excuses
- Show anger in email
- Blast out all your points in an opening conversation
- Say too much or use more emotional energy than necessary
- Point to your authority, experience, contract, or code of ethics before exhausting all other options
- Blame someone else
- Assign base motives
- Pin labels like "the board is toxic" or "he acts like a borderline"
- Go into deep analysis of how the situation came to be
- Try to win by showing how angry or appalled you are
- Cite confidential information to defend yourself

OPTIONS OF LAST RESORT

Consider using humor while keeping in mind that humor can be disarming or inflaming, or both at the same time. Generally, bring humor into conflict only as a Last Resort. Be mindful that anything you say will likely be repeated to others.

- "She insisted that Friday night service be at 7 p.m. instead of an earlier time. 'I've been a highly active member of this synagogue thirty years, and my experience here speaks volumes.' I responded with, 'That's some coincidence. I was ordained thirty years ago. That's a lot of experience between us.'"
- "After the organ broke, a proposed electronic keyboard upset some of our long-term members. When one of the opponents cited her length of membership as a valid reason to drop the idea and make the repair so that 'things stay as they were,' I asked, 'How long does someone need to belong here to get a veto on a new idea?'"

Take the anger a step higher

- "I know you think I did something wrong. How should I be punished?"
- "I hear you are unhappy with the educator, even though I think she is doing a good job. Do you want to fire her?"
- "I guess you are stuck with me through the end of my contract, if not longer."

EXPECT THINGS TO WORSEN UNTIL THEY IMPROVE

Expect emotions to run even higher as you turn to these options of Last Resort. You may feel even more "anxious" when you say these things, but do not let that impact your "presence." Realize that tension may continue to increase before calm returns. Rabbi Edwin Friedman drew an analogy to the experience of test pilots preparing to break the speed of sound. They found that, as jet speed approached the sound barrier, turbulence increased and raised the concern that the jet would break apart. Test pilot Chuck Yaeger correctly anticipated that once they passed the barrier, turbulence would end and smooth flying would return, and that is just what happened. Friedman compared that experience to what happens to emotions that rise until they stop rising. The atmosphere gets more agitated until things calm down and life returns to what it was. You might even want to provoke such a dust-up when the other side of the sound barrier is in sight.

> You must descend ever anew into the transforming abyss, risk your soul ever anew, ever anew vowed to the holy insecurity.[3]

In this chapter, we introduced and examined a Systems Theory Approach. The next chapter speaks to how NAP upholds Boundaries and manages Triangulation.

---

3. Buber, *Daniel*, 52.

11

The Skill of Upholding Boundaries

BOUNDARIES DEFINE ROLES, CLARIFY and establish limits, assign responsibility, and protect individual and congregational integrity. Boundaries can be rigid or flexible, closed or porous, or even enmeshed. They vary from person to person, across situations, and over time.

Empowerment and Boundaries work together, as they did in the Hebrew Bible. For example, Adam and Eve crossed a Boundary by eating the forbidden fruit of the tree of knowledge of good and evil. The transgression also Empowered them to "distinguish good and bad" (Gen 3).

Families, friends, society, and organizations function best with clear, appropriate, and livable boundaries. Boundaries serve congregations by protecting confidential pastoral and financial information. They establish clergy as responsible for determining the order of worship. A code of ethics and other documents set Boundaries for professional behavior. Boundaries protect the personal and private life of clergy just as they define areas of responsibility for other clergy in the congregation, staff, and leaders.

An Empowerment Approach trusts people to respect and uphold Boundaries. It extends the benefit of doubt until that trust is dishonored. Everyone, including clergy, crosses boundaries eventually, no matter how noble our intentions, ideals, or work ethic.

The Skill of Upholding Boundaries

And sometimes we violate one boundary to uphold another, for instance when sharing confidential information to protect a child's physical safety.

WHO OWNS WHAT

The congregation, for the most part, is "theirs." They were there before we arrived and will remain after we leave. The board functions as the fiduciary trustee of the congregation and ensures alignment of the congregation's work and vision. The board and committees generally hold authority over:

- Finance
- Property
- Program scheduling, other than the dates of set religious observances
- Worship service starting times and activities surrounding worship
- Establishing and upholding operational policies and documents
- Staff hiring, retention, and termination
- Election and appointment of leaders

When the leaders face decisions in such areas, clergy do well to hear out and weigh the concerns, assist in gathering information, encourage informed and thoughtful decision-making, and voice an opinion, if they have an opinion to voice. Clergy must respect and abide by the decision, even when they disagree. And some things just cannot be fixed.

> "Our finance officer of twenty years says he wants to hold the position for as long as he can. While he seems trustworthy, there was never an audit, and when I asked, he told me that it is not necessary. And he is very set in his ways. It took a long time, but I convinced him to turn payroll from paper checks to automatic deposit, but I

still haven't convinced him or the leaders to conduct any independent review. I wish I could bring in an auditor, but all I can do is continue to ask."

Entrenched leadership carries great sway.

"The long-time house chair works in construction. I noticed that the board approves repairs without competitive bidding. I questioned this and was told, 'Rabbi, butt out!' I did."

Sometimes, we find ourselves challenged to take a stand. Even as clergy are paid to enter the building, leaders pay for the privilege of volunteering. They "own" the congregation, and clergy can only exert limited influence.

CLERGY RESPONSIBILITIES

While specifics very among clergy and across congregations and denominations, clergy responsibilities include a small number of essential areas.

- Pulpit and ritual decisions and conduct, what to preach about, worship structure and process, and selection of liturgy. The cantor makes musical decisions.
- What to teach and how to teach it.
- Pastoral care protocols, schedule, and who is visited. Confidentiality is paramount, and access to pastoral care tracking should be limited.
- The content of pastoral conversations. While those who receive our counsel are free to report out, we are to avoid comment, even to the point of holding in confidence the names of those who seek us out and when we meet.
- Actual work hours. How long to spend at a hospital bedside, whether to go to a post-ceremony wedding reception or a congregant's home for dinner.

THE SKILL OF UPHOLDING BOUNDARIES

- The discretionary fund operations, except for a confidential audit
- The senior or sole clergy serves as the head of the staff for day-to-day operations
- Private behavior, including home and family life, and clergy health that does not impact performance
- The responsibility to uphold a code of ethics, denominational rules, written and verbal employment agreements
- Supporting personal boundaries for staff and leaders, such they are protected from being overextended, under-utilized, ignored, harassed, intimidated, abused, or required to undertake responsibilities beyond their assignments

WHEN BOUNDARIES ARE CROSSED

Congregations are composed of the public who behave consistently at home, work, with friends, and at the synagogue or church. People create the same situations in private, at meetings, at restaurants, and at the gym. In any congregation, a small number of folks seem to behave in ways that consume a disproportional amount of our time and energy, all too visible when they cross a Boundary.

The initial response to Boundary-crossing should be charitable. People are sad, lonely, or despairing, and they are entitled to the benefit of the doubt, at least at the outset. Some Boundary challenges rise from indifference, entitlement, or hostility. Others arise out of lack of clarity or confusion. These incidents, likely upsetting, are a call to remind ourselves that God's love extends to all, including those who we feel annoy us. We do well to remember that we have the resources to address, or at least mitigate, the impact of much of the behavior that we consider negative or harmful.

Addressing a problem begins by acknowledging that something is wrong and even this can be hard to do. A congregation's imperfection has a theological overtone. For instance, the Hebrew Bible teaches us to "serve God with joy" (Ps 100:2), so joylessness or anger in a sacred place is a spiritual failure, and no one wants to admit that they failed spiritually. Moreover, upholding a Boundary asks the clergy to shift from the role of a calming, pastoral presence to an assertive or even confrontational persona, which can be unfamiliar and uncomfortable. On top of all that, acknowledging failure is a call to action that places another headache onto an already overflowing schedule. It is much easier to convince oneself that "nothing will come of this, so nothing needs to be done," even while one is being eaten up over worry. A healthier approach sees self-compromise as an opportunity to summon NAP and speak as I-Thou. It relies on a realistic assessment and action plan that sustains the integrity of the clergy and the congregation.

To be sure, "caving in" is always an option when people act inappropriately, say, by spouting an extreme measure of anger disproportional to the matter at hand. However, the optics around immediate yielding to an over-the-top emotional outburst create an impression that acting that way gets what you want. It incentivizes the expression of outrage, hurt, or weakness as a strategy to commandeer policy or practice to the detriment of the organization, mission, and objectives, or the private life of the clergy.

> "My predecessor gave in to people. The word must have been out that if you yell or pressure, you will get whatever you want. When I arrived, people pushed me to do things that I said no to. They kept pushing, got angry, and expected me to yield, but I never did and each one of those problems eventually went away. The people behaved more civilly. You can hold your ground like that, as an interim, and when you do, you make it easier for your successor. Let me tell you that my successor was very grateful to me."

If your predecessor had a habit of letting things pass without reacting or even commenting, you may be inheriting an expectation that you will be just as passive. Hard as it is to assert oneself, it becomes harder to break a pattern that should never have been there from the start.

The Skill of Upholding Boundaries

Boundary enforcement often adds flame to an already inflamed situation, making people even angrier. As discussed, raising short-term anxiety can serve a greater, long-term peace when things get worse before improving.

Once a Boundary-crossing is recognized and labeled, we turn to general approaches.

ALLOCATE PROPER RESPONSIBILITY

Many Boundary crossings can be addressed by sending the problem to the proper person or body. For instance, a complaint about a Sunday school teacher properly goes to the teacher first, then the principal. In other words, the clergy or the president should not be the first one to hear and certainly not the first to react. Questions about building rental and use, billing, publicity, and finance go through the executive director or front office, not the clergy.

- "You should speak to the Sunday school teacher first."
- "Let's bring this to the board."
- "I'd like to involve the education committee."

For policy matters,

> "I don't blame you for being upset. This is a question of congregational policy and should be decided by the committee. I'll find out when the committee meets and get back to you."

You can, but do not have to, make the referral yourself.

> "Our educator should be the first to hear this. Please talk to him. I find him very responsive. If you are not happy, then please come back to me and I will follow up."

In a synagogue with a cantor, music suggestions go there.

- "I'm familiar with the version of the *Sh'ma* that you like. I know that the cantor chose to sing something else. Let me ask you to please raise this with the cantor. She is the musical

- expert and would be happy to hear from you. You should know that I like what she does."
- "I understand that you have an issue with the selection of the music. I appreciate what the cantor chooses, but that doesn't mean you have to. But you must raise that with him. He makes musical decisions."

Sometimes the clergy must hold their ground.

> "I told him I decided which prayers to say. I welcome comments from the congregation, but the decision of the order of the liturgy is my responsibility as the senior clergy of the congregation."

Use Boundary descriptions to keep folks responsible.

> "No, ordering religious school materials is your job as office manager. It is not the job of the school director."

Encourage people to take ownership of what is theirs instead of Offloading their responsibility on you or others.

> "I told my educator that I can talk to the cantor about a school issue. But the best thing is person-to-person communication between the two of them rather than jumping to include a third party."

A committee may exceed its mandate.

> "The environment committee is insisting on a Sunday school-wide session for the environment. The calendar is packed, and we would have to cancel something else to accommodate this request. The committee chairs must hammer this out."

Offer support without taking full responsibility:

> "Some of the religious school parents wanted the service to start earlier and they asked me to make the change on my own. I told them that this was up to the ritual committee, and I added that if they take the lead, I will go with them and support the request."

THE SKILL OF UPHOLDING BOUNDARIES
PIVOT FROM CONTENT TO PROCESS

The Pivot from Content to Process turns attention from the *facts* under discussion to the *manner* of discussion. You can put out many fires by redirecting a conversation away from the things themselves to how they are properly deliberated and decided. Let's say a congregant complains that your sermon on gay rights was "political," and you respond by defending the content.

- "That was about social justice, not politics."
- "That was about faith teachings, not politics."
- "I can preach about whatever I want to preach about, including politics, as a matter of freedom of the pulpit."
- "Let me tell you why you are wrong and I am right."

These responses sound defensive because they are. Avoid getting into a "talk show" argument by defending the Content of what you are saying or upholding your "right" to say it. You will lose. Instead, Pivot to the Process by pointing to what is going on between the two of you at that moment. React with Parsimony:

- "We sure do disagree!"
- "We each feel strongly!"
- "We certainly look at this issue differently!"

Deflate by adding, "And that is OK. People have all kinds of opinions. We have this in the congregation all the time. And we find it everywhere else." If the criticism persists, do not argue Content. Stay on your Pivot to Process. Acknowledge that there is a difference of opinion and that you will allow the difference to stand.

- "I recognize that we do not look at the issue the same way. That is just how it is sometimes. I know it is upsetting."
- "I wish we could agree on everything, but as you look around the sanctuary and look a little deeper, we see that opinions in the congregation differ."

- "I think we can agree that there is no easy way to resolve this difference, and we must let it stand for now. I wish we could do better than that, but I don't see a better way right now."
- "We disagree with each other just as we disagree with friends, neighbors, and family members. There are also disagreements in the congregation. Just as you and I have family, we love each other, even when we disagree. And I hope we can do the same at this church."

ESCALATE WITH PARSIMONY BY POINTING TO PROCESS ERRORS

As upset increases, the likelihood of inappropriate behavior also increases. You will prevail as NAP if you react thoughtfully when someone tells you, "Anyone with common sense can see that I am right."

One of my mentors, Rabbi Michael Robinson, said, "Stay calm! When people are angry at you, they give you power over them. Use it!" Someone who goes into a rage will likely breach the Process and provide an opportunity. A process breach could include sidelining those responsible (A committee, other clergy, staffer) or involving third parties that have no responsibility for a situation. Pivot from Content to Process by asking things like:

- "I told him this is a worship committee matter. Why did he leapfrog over the committee by writing the entire board?"
- "He certainly has a right to suggest that idea and feel very strongly about it. My issue is how he raised the concern by personally attacking the clergy."
- "I respect what you think about how I decide pulpit matters. That is not the issue. The issue is that I found out about it from someone else. You should have come right to me."

Be honest about the Pivot from Content to Process. Underscore that your issue is not the material of the complaint, how upset people get, or anyone's right to complain. Stress that people have a right to believe as they do, even when opinions differ. The issue is over the proper forum and protocol for expressing deeply held opinions. You will appear confident and gracious by encouraging respectful behavior.

MANAGING CONFLICTS OF INTEREST

Place Boundary crossings in a context of "conflict of interests" rather than "all or nothing." Clergy have multiple clients, including the board, individual members, committees, staff, and themselves. Clergy also deal with multiple clients when families compete for a wedding date, when a proposed funeral time conflicts with a scheduled congregational program, or a sitting interim is asked to honor a request from a designated successor that goes against their own sense of what is best for the congregation. Multiple clients create multiple roles that impose multiple and conflicting responsibilities. When goods compete, someone, such as the clergy, must decide which good to honor. Be prepared that someone will come away frustrated, fail to see the clergy caught in the middle, take the matter in personal terms, and blame the clergy.

There can be a Conflict of Interests when it comes to protecting safety and upholding confidentiality.

> "The child got hurt at school and asked me not to tell the parent. Instead of saying an outright 'no!,' I said I wished I could keep that a secret but that I also have a responsibility to ensure that everyone is safe here."

When it comes to contract negotiation,

> "Yes, I have a responsibility to support the congregation's financial solvency. On the other hand, I cannot live on this salary, as much as I wish I could. I understand the congregation's position, and I hope the congregation understands mine."

The conflicts can be intense, especially in smaller congregations, when members are considered for the staff.

> "I wanted the temple to hire a cantor, but a board member was promoting their adult child to serve as a soloist. I was hearing, 'Why pay an outsider when one of us, who receives so many compliments, is available?' I said that I love to work with their daughter, but we need someone with formal musical training and Jewish knowledge."

Awards for student excellence also stir emotions when a child of a leader is under consideration.

> "When the committee conversation turned to finding a student to receive a college scholarship, an officer, whose child was nominated, decided to recuse themselves, fortunately!"

Other ways to say "no":

- "On the one hand, I want to help you. On the other, where would the money come from?"
- "Yes, I recognize the committee wants the concert on that date. But we have another event scheduled, and planning has moved forward on that other event. I am caught in the middle. What do we do?"

"CAN I ASK A QUICK QUESTION?"

It happens at the restroom entrance or right after a meeting when a full response is not possible, when you get a "quick question" that involves a "long answer."

> "I was on my way out of the church when a member stopped me with 'can I ask a quick question?' and without missing a beat said to me, 'I am retiring and would like your suggestions as to what I could do for the church.' I said that I would welcome the opportunity to sit down and talk more deeply, but the member went on. I was insistent until the member agreed. I later emailed to set up an appointment where we had a good discussion about what it feels like to retire and the options for church volunteering."

The Skill of Upholding Boundaries

The parking lot is a popular venue.

> "At curbside Sunday school drop-off, a parent shouted through the open car window, holding up the rest of the line to ask, 'My child needs to skip three weeks of religious school. Can he do makeup?' I said I would let the educator know and that one of us would be back in touch."

It is important to set limits on "quick questions" that involve controversial matters.

> "It was right after the bat mitzvah, as I was heading to my office to go home, when a member of the family, someone I never met before, came up to me to complain, 'Nice service, rabbi. But I have a problem with Israel.' I told him that this was not a good time for me to talk about this. He responded, 'I know Israel was attacked, but their response is over the top.' I repeated myself and then I turned the conversation to another topic by asking him where he was from and how he is related to the family."

"I WILL QUIT IF . . . !"

Threats of "I will quit unless I get my way" or "you can expect me to cut my pledge if that policy goes forward" are common. Sometimes people threaten and back down, while other times they threaten and have no intention of acting on the threat. And sometimes people will follow through.

Retain your dignity. Avoid begging or looking frightened. Appeal to the larger picture and mission:

> "I know this is important to you. But this is a moment when we must come together for the benefit of the congregation."

Personnel matters are especially provocative.

> "I am also upset that the board did not renew the cantor's contract. But being part of a congregation means making peace when the majority vote does not go our way."

Pastor to the Body of the Congregation

PASTORAL CARE BOUNDARIES

Our members will use email to ask their clergy about personal matters. Avoid email responses to pastoral inquiries that could be misinterpreted, provoke upset, or get forwarded to others without your consent.

> "We met in my study to discuss his complicated medical situation. The next day he emailed that he had one more question, which had to do with his sister's conversion into another religion. I told him that I wanted a thorough understanding of the situation and that I would welcome another in person conversation. He never got back to me."

Consider Boundaries when confronted by awkward situations over officiating.

> "Following the chapel memorial, we reached the cemetery and a couple I did not know approached and said, 'The deceased had a brother. Why didn't you mention that from the pulpit? You need to say something at graveside.' I told them that I had no idea and that I was sorry for their loss. But I worked for the family members that belong to the congregation, and I take their direction. 'You have to raise this concern with them.'"

Here, another heartbreaking situation became further compounded when divorced parents disagreed over the funeral service for their adult child.

> "When he told me that he and his ex did not agree on several important ceremony details, I called her on the spot. The three of us talked and we worked everything out."

Later, we will talk more deeply about upholding Boundaries after leaving a congregation. Here:

> "A week after I left the congregation, a member called to ask my opinion about an ongoing family matter that I was familiar with and had been supportive. I said, 'I hope

the situation settles down, but I must ask you to contact your new rabbi. That rabbi is the one to help you.'"

Show an appropriate amount of care without crossing a line.

PRIORITIZE SAFETY

Safeguarding the safety of property and person is paramount. A threat against anyone on the staff or any member is a threat to everyone. When counseling in your study, consider these suggestions:

- Sit with access to an exit
- Keep heavy or sharp objects out of sight
- Meet only when others are in the building
- Let the office know when and where you are paying a home visit
- Get a phone number, address, and email address when making appointments with folks you've never met before
- Your office door should have a glass window so people can see in.

Follow your instincts when you have a concern about personal safety.

LIMIT AN ANGRY EMAIL EXCHANGE

Offer to speak:

- Put enough information to show where you stand without attacking
- No more than two volleys before insisting on a call or in-person conversation
- Recognize that whatever you write can be forwarded

UPHOLD PERSONAL BOUNDARIES WITH PARSIMONY

Hold your ground when you meet them[1]

We uphold personal and professional Boundaries in the same way. A simple and polite "I" statement is often enough to set a limit. Avoid offering extended explanations that make you appear awkward, defensive, or imposed upon. Reveal as little personal information as possible.

- "I wish I could meet you for lunch, but I need to stay in the building all day."
- "I'm sorry I can't schedule the meeting then. I'm tied up all evening."
- "I would go to the preschool program, but the time is not good for me."
- "It took me a long time to make that doctor's appointment, and I didn't want to reschedule. I just said that I couldn't be at the meeting at that time, without giving an explanation, and I offered them several other time options."

Receptions after life cycle events, especially when the faith teaches that the meal is part of the ceremony, pose complications. Clergy may be unable or not wanting to stay. Again, decline and express regrets without providing details or making excuses.

---

1. Buber, *I and Thou*, 43.

The Skill of Upholding Boundaries

"I simply said that I was sorry I could not stay for the after-wedding reception. I was happy to be with them for the ceremony, but I would need to run afterwards."

Be clear about the spouse.

"I am sorry to say that my spouse cannot join us for the reception."

Offer to stay for a short period.

"I can stay for the cocktail hour but will have to leave before dinner."

Point to a previous commitment.

"I wish we could join you for dinner, but we already have something on the calendar."

Give them another option, if possible or desirable, and let them decide what is best for them.

"No, I can't meet with the committee on Tuesday. I am not available. I can meet any other day, except for Thursday."

Provide Appropriate Pastoral Attention

You may be in the middle of a conflict with someone who faces a pastoral need. NAP provides proper attention, separate from the issue.

"The day after he complained to the board about me in writing, I heard he had a recurrence, so I called to wish him good health. But I got off the phone as fast as I could. I wasn't going to say or ask anything about the temple."

Give Yourself Credit for What You Already Do

Lead with your strengths. When upholding a Boundary stirs discomfort or feelings of inadequacy, draw confidence from thinking about the times that you stood firm in the past with family, friends, and at work.

Pay Attention to Yourself

The body may speak before the mind when someone violates your Boundary. Note the visceral discomfort that says something is not right.

> "I was taught to go with my gut, to pay attention to how I feel."

Finally, given the centrality of our congregations in the lives of our members, we should not be surprised that they get upset. A long time member reflected,

> "When I came to that event the other night that honored us 'seniors,' I felt I achieved something with my life. The congregation has been here for forty years, and I was here from the start. This place is making a difference, and all this happens because of me."

The ability to recognize and uphold Boundaries is an essential Systems Theory Approach skill. Now we turn to the skills of managing Triangulation as NAP, skills at the heart of a Systems Theory Approach.

12

The Skills of Recognizing and Addressing Triangulation

WHAT IS TRIANGULATION?

Triangulation happens when two people turn to a third person or an issue. Triangulation begins at birth and is a normal and healthy part of human life. Parents Triangulate to care for a child. Parents and teachers Triangulate at Open School Night to discuss the child's progress. A boss and worker Triangulate to plan out a productive schedule. We humans, social beings, come into our full selves through these kinds of interactions.

Triangulation in the congregation is good when:

- A member calls to tell the pastor someone is sick
- The leaders and rabbi meet to plan to support an underperforming staff member
- A teen's parents are excited to meet with the cantor to discuss an upcoming bat mitzvah service
- Out of upset that the current format is not working, the educator and minister plan family worship

For all the times Triangulation advances the quality of life, it can be troublesome when:

- A member and the cantor trade complaints about the rabbi
- The priest and the office manager swap gossip about a church leader
- Church members at a poker game share stories about the pastor not being much of a pastor
- The rabbi and the custodian let off steam about the executive director
- A parent calls the president to accuse the cantor of playing favorites when assigning b'nai mitzvah dates
- A board member who criticized the president at a board meeting invites the minister to lunch
- A school committee meeting descends into a big argument when some parents gang up to criticize a teacher and other parents rise to the teacher's defense

Triangulation can be emotionally seductive or aggressive, sometimes both simultaneously.

> "Our caring committee is a great help when they tell me that someone wants to see me. On one hand, the chair is very complimentary of my response time, such that I got suspicious. Then, someone told me that she was complaining that I keep too much to myself, such as who I call, when I call, when I visit, and for how long. Later, I learned that the chair sometimes checks in on me by calling the members to find out whether I visited and what happened. The compliments keep coming, but I am waiting for a problem to pop up."

Signs of seductive Triangulation include:

- People who befriend too quickly or too early
- Praise beyond what is earned or deserved
- When you sense there is an ulterior motive behind a compliment or an invitation

Recognizing and Addressing Triangulation

When it comes to Triangulation, think of the potential to turn I-It to I-Thou.

TRIANGLES BEGIN WITH ANXIETY

Triangulating behaviors begin with anxiety, a catchall term for worry, fear, and attraction. Anxiety brings people together with the hope of finding calm, reassurance, or self-confidence. People also Triangulate to experience *Schadenfreude*. The German word Schadenfreude describes the pleasure that comes from witnessing someone else be humiliated, made anxious, or have a hard time, especially when that person is perceived to deserve punishment. There's Schadenfreude, akin to gloating, in the office, the morning after the "big game" in the teasing, "My team won and yours lost."

It is ironic to suggest that Schadenfreude lives in a caring community that, as a matter of faith, should comfort and help people in need instead of delighting in their affliction. A particular brand of Schadenfreude rises when the pastor squirms.

- "Even though she knew that I am working on a stronger pulpit presence, she smiled when she told me that someone had again complained to her about my sermon."
- "I had already given notice that I was leaving, and he came in to ask for a donation from my discretionary fund to support a cause that they knew gave me mixed feelings. He and I never got along, so I smiled and said that I would be leaving in a month and would leave money for the next rabbi to decide what to do."

Whatever motivates Triangulation, clergy, especially interims, need a working understanding of what Triangles are, what drives them, how to recognize them, and, how to take advantage of them or overcome them.

People Triangulate when:

- Feeling a compulsion to be right
- Worried about being supplanted by a colleague

- Seeing others take credit for their work or are unwilling or incapable of giving others credit for their own success
- Refusing to admit mistakes or apologize
- Unable to let go of grudges or guilt
- Others, including the clergy, usurp their limelight
- Perceiving a loss of standing in the eyes of others
- Feeling ashamed
- Seeking approval or attention
- Sensing a disparity between how the group values them and how they think they should be valued
- Feeling underappreciated for all they do for the congregation
- Seeking to avenge perceived embarrassment
- Hearing rumors that they do not do good work for the congregation
- Wanting to avoid looking inadequate
- Seeking to prove that they are as smart, if not smarter, than others
- Desiring special accommodation worthy of their sense of entitlement
- Advocating on behalf of someone else who is upset or who they think has been treated dismissively.
- Shifting blame to someone else
- Feeling romantic or wanting to get close to another

Particularly problematic Triangulation is seen in behaviors that:

- Disparage others
- Jump to criticize
- Prioritize one's right to speak at the expense of others
- Jump to conclusions without hearing out alternatives
- Reach decisions with no intention to follow up

Recognizing and Addressing Triangulation

- Attack the integrity of the clergy or another leader
- Demonstrate binary either/or thinking without seeking a middle ground
- Withhold sharing an opinion for fear of getting someone angry or disappointed
- Are intended to pursue an inappropriate relationship

Clergy also Triangulate when feeling:

- Frightened
- Anxious
- Angry
- Unguarded
- Resisting change
- Avoiding involvement
- Seeking someone's attention just for the sake of seeking it
- Revealing confidential information to avoid being blamed for failure or to cement a friendship
- Lonely

Again, some Triangulation is positive, as when clergy seek to advance a consensus agenda. Clergy Triangulate to:

- Sustain strength
- Effect a positive change
- Have an honest relationship

You are in the Triangle's Lone Corner if you:

- Cannot understand why people are so upset about something so insignificant
- React disproportionally to the issue
- See blame placed on your spouse or children

- See one person working multiple triangles against you (school parents, choir, house committee) and the triangles spread a negative message
- Are hopeful that a problem will go away, without any logical basis for that hope
- Feel powerless and unable to respond to a Demand for Work
- Feel anxious, and people appear to be glad you are upset

RECOGNIZING TYPES OF TRIANGULATIONS: ILLUSION OF WORK

An Illusion of Work[1] describes some forms of Triangulation. An Illusion of Work gives the impression that something productive is happening while nothing meaningful occurs. It is in going through motions that provide self-assurance that constructive work is being done, even though everything stays the same. A lot happens but nothing changes under the Illusion of Work.

An Illusion of Work is evident in sticking to a monthly meeting out of a duty to meet, even when there are no agenda items. More than that, the meeting must not end early. It must go on for at least an hour to justify asking everyone to come. And at the end of the meeting, even though nothing happened beyond the conversation, another meeting is scheduled. "All we do is meet with ourselves," remarked one observer.

> "The meeting went on for an hour. They didn't stick to the topic and had no agenda. It felt like a night out for a gripe session rather than a business meeting. No one assigned any work or volunteered to follow up. I just sat through it and spoke, just once, to agree with something someone said."

An Illusion of Work appears in a rehash of old or irrelevant arguments that attempt to explain away an awkward situation by telling you what you already know. Or, when a conversation goes

1. Shulman, *Skills of Helping Individuals*, 110.

in an uncomfortable direction, an Illusion of Work turns the discussion to a less provocative topic, and the original matter remains unresolved. It is in unsolicited advice and in second-hand complaints. Under an Illusion of Work, a lot gets said but very little changes.

Through an Illusion of Work, the speaker convinces themself that they are contributing to the cause while avoiding a hard conversation about something hurtful (removing a popular pastor) or overwhelming (selling the property). Merely talking is a way to show oneself that they are competent and in control, smarter than others, or at least not less intelligent. Nothing has changed other than the people have spoken. Everything stays as it was, problem and all.

The Illusion of Work can take many forms.

Default Responses

A Default Response is an oft-cited refrain invoked after repeated mention of an ongoing challenge. An event or situation triggers the same response, with the hope that the complainer will go away and take their complaint with them. The Default Response:

- Deflects attention from the problem
- As an Illusion of Work, gives the impression that the speaker is educating the listener about why this problem will not improve
- Showcases one's expertise
- Demonstrates being in control
- Adds no new information to what the listener already knows
- Triangulates by putting the topic of discussion and/or the person being addressed in the Lone Corner

    As examples of Default Responses, when the question is:

- "Why don't families with children come to services?," the Default Response is, "You know how those young families are!"

Pastor to the Body of the Congregation

instead of saying, "I'm calling a few of them to invite them to come."

- "Why do we always let him get away with behaving like that?," the Default Response is, "That's just the way he is. He's always angry," instead of saying, "I will call him and start a friendly conversation about his conduct."

- "I keep asking why we need to hunt down two signatures for a check as small as $100?," the Default Response is, "The By-laws committee will address that," instead of saying, "I'll call a meeting of the bylaws committee next Monday evening, and I will send out invites."

- "Why can't we start the service thirty minutes earlier? People have been asking for a while," the Default Response is, "Those older members don't want anything to change," instead of saying, "I'll get a few folks together and see what we can do."

If you are receiving a Default Response, you can also say, and repeat, "I didn't ask why we have the problem. I am looking for a way for us to address the problem."

Grandstanding

Grandstanding is in a self-promoting and exaggerated response to a minor problem. Rather than pursue a simpler, more efficient, and less attention-grabbing path by acting with Parsimony, Grandstanding is an Illusion of Work that says, "I want everyone aware of this outrage!" in a way that highlights the Grandstander's nobility, experience, wisdom, or sacrifice rather than the problem.

Grandstanding occurs when someone springs new business on the board without any committee or executive foreknowledge, review, or recommendation because "the board should know this, NOW!" Grandstanding Triangulation puts the topic, and/or the bullied person, in the Lone Corner.

You can head off Grandstanding.

"In advance of a committee meeting, the chair threatened that 'there will be fireworks' if the meeting didn't go in a particular way. I asked, 'Why do we need fireworks?' and the chair dropped the matter."

Address Grandstanding when blindsighted.

"I wish you had told me about this beforehand. We could have resolved it without upending a meeting and taking the time of all these good people."

Protect yourself after a Grandstanding event by reaching out to the Grandstander:

"The committee chair went to the board without telling me, accusing me of bypassing the committee to organize a teen travel program. This took up twenty minutes of board time. Nothing came of it. The next day, the chair refused my invitation to come in and talk it over. But I never had another problem with this leader."

Information Management

Information is one of the most important congregational resources. Controlling information—what, who knows, how much they know, who should not know—is fertile soil for Triangulation. The information—and/or the person who is deceived and/or denied information—is in the Lone Corner. Information Management and mismanagement includes:

Distorted Truth

Failures are exaggerated and successes downplayed or underreported. Small lies, understatements, and misrepresentations muddy the facts.

"I can't believe he called the president to say I refused to meet with him because I was too busy. I said that I have an obligation Tuesday morning, but I can meet Tuesday afternoon. He hung up on me."

Withheld Information

Withheld information is in the intentional concealment of facts. It is in a failure to inform clergy about a pastoral request that trap the clergy into receiving blame for inattentiveness. "No one ever told me. How should I have known to be there?"

Information Is Wrongly Shared

Truthful information goes to a person that should not receive it. Confidential financial information is passed to clergy, or confidential pastoral information goes to a congregational leader, perhaps as a way of building a personal relationship with the listener.

Nostalgia

Nostalgia is a warmly remembered past. It speaks of recapturing something no longer available. It is triggered by a negative perception of the present that puts "here and now" and/or the listener in the Lone Corner. The Default Response of bringing up "the good old days" serves as an Illusion of Work that educates the minister with what is inaccessible and unachievable. Nostalgia says, "The present is dissatisfying, and we cannot go back, so there is nothing we can do. You are unable to help me." The best response to Nostalgia is in Leading with Strengths and developing a work plan.

Offloading

Offloading places one person's problem on someone else, who then winds up in the Lone Corner. As an Illusion of Work, it suggests that a problem was fully addressed.

- "Having had enough of hearing 'let the youth group do it' and seeing the work not happen, I assured them that it was fine to ask the teens but to also have a backup plan in place in case the teens would be unavailable."

- "The confirmation class parent complained to me that the class, with six kids, was too small and wanted to know 'what are we doing to make it bigger?,' I said we are doing what we can and suggested that the parents reach out to families of other prospective students. 'Please help us spread the good word!'"

Second-Hand Complaints

A Second-Hand Complaint conveys someone else's problem. It communicates a grievance that could have been more efficiently expressed through direct communication by the upset party. Passing along a Second-Hand Complaint creates an Illusion of Work by giving the appearance that the messenger is acting responsibly, when, in fact, responsible behavior would have been to tell the person who started this chain to go right to the person (such as the clergy, who is placed in the Lone Corner) that upsets them. The messenger thinks this is I-Thou, but it really is I-It.

Lodging a Second-Hand Complaint, though self-touted as noble, undermines the integrity of communication in a congregation. Note that the originator of the complaint may have wanted the complaint to be held confidential. A Second-Hand Complaint is a common and challenging Triangulation.

As an Illusion of Work, it:

- Allows for pseudo self-congratulation for the bravery to speak up and do something that no one else did: "I was the only one with enough nerve to talk to the rabbi! Go me!"
- Allows for plausible deniability: "I'm just telling you what I hear people saying."

Respond to Second-Hand Complaints with Parsimony by asking to speak directly to the source of the complaint. You will likely hear something like "they asked me not to tell you who they are." Whether the complainer wishes to be known or anonymous, the responses are the same.

Get the messenger out of the middle. You can say:

- "I accept that people are saying what you are telling me. Please tell me who they are. I know they don't want to be identified. I need to speak to them directly, so they know I care about them and what they think."
- "If people are upset with something I did, they should raise it first with me. Then, if they are unhappy with my response, it is perfectly appropriate for them to go to the leaders."
- "I appreciate your concern, but I encourage people to speak for themselves. Can you ask them to contact me, or can I call them?"
- "You say, 'People are upset?' Exactly how many people spoke to you about this?"
- "Let me get you out of the middle. I'd like to make your life easier. Let me speak directly to that person."
- "What do *you* think about the complaint?"
- "I hear what you are saying, but I care about this person. I am their clergy, and they are my congregant. I want to get to know them. Please help me be the pastor here."

Go from general to specific. Second-Hand Complaints are often vague and lack detail. Ask pointed questions to help the bearer realize they do not have the information they should have. This can end the complaint for good.

- "Which parts of my sermon troubled them the most?"
- "We had several names read for healing. Which one did I mispronounce? And maybe I can visit them."
- "I was talking to someone else, and I did not realize they were waiting to talk to me. Help me figure out when this happened. Who was I talking to?"
- "I understand that people are saying such things. I'd like to hear more of your own thoughts on the issue."

Recognizing and Addressing Triangulation

Go from specific to general:

- "I can understand that someone would complain about something I said at a pastoral visit. Do you see this as an overall problem on my part?"
- "How often do you really hear this?"

Ask the messenger to help:

- "Please do me a favor. Please tell them that you spoke to me and that we both feel they need to talk to me."
- "You help everyone by telling them they have incorrect information and that I would be happy to talk to them."

Underscore your pastoral responsibility to an unhappy congregant. You want to hear directly from them and demonstrate open communication with your members. No one should get in the way of the relationship between the faithful and their religious leaders.

Taking Opinion as Fact

Committee discussions raise speculation intended to be taken as actionable truth. As an Illusion of Work, Taking Opinion as Fact allows the speaker, who proposes a "quick fix" to a troublesome issue, to think they solved the problem.

- "The preschool was suffering from a lack of enrollment and loss of revenue. It has been a money loser for years; the situation was getting worse. When we were discussing closure, a leader offered, 'I am convinced there are people out there who will send their kids. We can very easily find them.' I had a lot of trouble getting that leader to realize we already exhausted that route."
- "Why hire someone to do that job? If we put something in the bulletin, I am sure we will get volunteers to step up. We can save a ton of money!"

- "Why are we wasting time and money to pay someone to set up our office computers? There must be a teen in the congregation who knows about computers to help us. Kids are experts in this."

"Opinion" includes wild accusations that have no basis in fact.

> "If this synagogue dies, it will be because of you. You are only an interim, and you do not care about this place."

Rebutting wild accusations only fuels them. Moreover, it delegates control of the argument to the accuser. Instead of responding with facts, take control of an agitated conversation by pivoting to another topic or ignoring the statement.

OTHER FORMS OF TRIANGULATION

Bullying

Bullying, as Triangulation, involves three individuals or separate groups—bully, victim, and enabler. The bully is astute enough to identify a victim as someone who will passively stay in the Lone Corner and endure aggression. The enabler is a silently complicit staffer, leader, or committee that has the wherewithal to prevent Bullying but does nothing.

- "His unhappiness about how I treated his seventh grader simmered until it boiled over in the parking lot after a meeting when he threatened that I would have a 'political problem' if things continued as they were going."
- "A leader, lacking any official responsibility for the building or the staff, told the custodian that he would lose his job unless he prepared the room in a particular way."
- "A member with a history of aggressive behavior to me and to others barged into my office and demanded that I supervise the educator more forcefully. I responded, 'No one here works for you.' The member got up and left, and I never heard about this matter again."

- "The parent sat in my study and said that many families were upset with the later b'nai mitzvah service start time. She mentioned a few, some of whom I knew did not agree with her. I said I needed to hear from them before I consider the next step."

Bullying is particularly intimidating when, in a "game of smoke and mirrors," the bully purports to speak for others when they only speak for themselves. A bully may reference others by name when there was never a conversation.

Bullies will enlist others as allies or deputies to do their bullying for them.

- "The member yelled at me because the temple fired her neighbor's son for being a poor custodian; I held my ground. So, she convinced a board member to come in to see me to accuse me of being a 'lousy rabbi.' I just shrugged. The matter then dropped from sight."

- "I never caught the emeritus complaining about me. But I got plenty of word of what his spouse said to others against me."

When questioned about their inaction, an enabler will respond, "I know he's a lousy office manager, and he can be hard to take sometimes. But:

- "The temple will lose members and money if he leaves."
- "He knows where everything is and who everyone is."
- "We can't function without him."
- "He works so hard. No one else will do that job."
- "He is, nevertheless, very popular among members who do not know the inside story. They will leave the church if we fire him."

You can break up the Bully-Victim-Enabler Triangle merely by threatening to involve others. Shine light on the situation, and call the bully's bluff.

- "Let's have the board decide."
- "This is a committee matter."
- "Let's schedule a meeting with the cantor to get to the bottom of this."
- "This is not my responsibility. Who can we invite into our conversation?"

Fast Friends

Fast Friends jump out as soon as you arrive, if not sooner. That dinner invitation may be an honest attempt to start up a relationship that will last a good long time, so offer an initial benefit of the doubt. Or it may mark an effort to "recruit" you for some political cause. Or it can be a seductive attempt to Triangulate by establishing a privileged relationship with the clergy that feeds the urge to boast, "Oh, yes. We had another dinner at the rabbi's house. What a lovely family," which leaves others feeling marginalized. Or it could blossom into an attempt to garner special consideration for themselves or their children.

Withhold initial suspicion. After all, they are our congregants, even if their actions will put the rest of the membership in the Lone Corner. It may turn out to be I-Thou. And keep in mind that we do not have to return any dinner invitations.

Feigned Powerlessness

Feigned Powerlessness is in pretending to lack the authority or ability to address an issue. It avoids confrontation by acting as if a situation is beyond one's bailiwick or capacity. The problem or speaker is in the Lone Corner.

Default Responses demonstrating Feigned Powerlessness include:

- "He doesn't listen to anyone."
- "I can't control him."
- "It never worked before, so it won't work now."
- "This is how it's always been."
- "Our congregation is willing to merge, but the other congregation is not."

Responses include:

- "Let's put our heads together, and see what we can do."
- "Has anyone ever raised this at the committee level?"
- "Maybe we can brainstorm and find a way to move forward."

Gaslighting

Gaslighting brings a person to question their judgment or self-esteem. A Gaslit person second-guesses themselves after taking to heart someone else's negative comment. Repeated Gaslighting can be a spiritual corrosive that accumulates over time. The Gaslit person is in the Lone Corner.

Gaslighting behaviors include:

- Questioning the integrity of what someone says:
    » "What you say makes no sense!"
    » "Do you really expect me to believe that?"

- Disparaging another's feelings:
    » "You are overreacting."
    » "You are trivializing."

- Denying the past:
    » "No, you never said that!"
    » "No, it didn't happen that way!"

- Accusing someone of being inadequate or incompetent:
  - » "Why do you let the temple leaders make so many decisions? Stand up for yourself!"
  - » "Letting people call you by your first name reduces your authority."
- Accusing someone of allowing themselves to be bullied: "The cantor has a stronger pulpit presence than you do. Why do you allow her to outshine you?"
- Denying another's authority: "Who gave you the right to make that decision?"

You may be Gaslit if you find yourself:

- Apologizing a lot
- Reluctant to talk to someone you perceive as aggressive
- Indecisive

Protect and defend yourself.

- Limit contact with those who Gaslight
- Keep to your story. Focus on what you want to say, not on what they are telling you.
- Speak with Parsimony in an "I" statement. Say no more than:
  - » "I look at it differently."
  - » "Let me think about it."
  - » "In a situation like this, I find it helpful to bring in another perspective."
  - » "I'm looking at the same elephant as you, and I guess we are seeing two different parts."

Gatekeeping

Gatekeeping is in a seemingly neutral statement or behavior intended to shut down a conversation, provoke an angry response, or seduce.[2] Gatekeeping is a subtle, incremental but aggressive or seductive step to encourage another person to do speak, act, or stop what they are doing. It is in a calculated statement or provocative question that opens the door for someone else to act and escalate the situation.

Aggressive Gatekeeping comments include:

- "The capital campaign is faltering. I wonder what the minister has to say."
- "Service attendance is down, and the rabbi has been giving lectures instead of preaching."
- "Someone is in the hospital, and they told me that the pastor have not called or visited."
- "The cantor is late again."
- "You leave your car overnight at the church."
- "You have a big banner outside the church that says, 'Warm, welcoming, and inclusive,' but some people feel out of place here."

Seductive Gatekeeping comments can be in:

- "You are the best rabbi we could ever have."
- "Text me when you get home, rabbi, so I know you arrived safely."
- "I hope you like this birthday present."

Just as Gatekeeping can open a conversation, it also shuts down a conversation that is uncomfortable.

- "We need to talk about something else."

---

2. Shulman, *Skills of Helping Individuals*, 565.

- "The time is late, and we can deal with this issue at our next meeting."
- "I need more information before we can talk further."

Gatekeeping comments are framed cagily to provide plausible deniability. An ostensibly neutral statement carves out enough "wiggle room" to shirk responsibility for what was said. Once confronted, the Gatekeeper walks back the comment with:

- "All I did was suggest something."
- "I'm just telling you what others say."
- "I just made a statement."
- "I'm only saying what I see."

A few words, spoken without anger or sounding defensive, can address Gatekeeping:

- "So?" (repeat as necessary)
- "And?" (repeat as necessary)
- "Yes, that is true."
- "Let me think about that."

Railroading

Railroading happens when someone brings up new business at a meeting without warning. By railroading, a person tries to get their way without having a full discussion. When confronted, someone doing the Blind Sighting may say, "My idea is so good that everyone would agree with it" or "What other people think is irrelevant. Given my insight, history of leadership, and generosity to the congregation, everyone should agree with me." Or "I am an expert on this, and I don't need anyone to tell me otherwise." It leapfrogs over the due process by rushing to an on-the-spot decision.

- "The treasurer, unhappy with the High Holiday ticket policy, sprung a proposal on the board. The president, for reasons I could not explain, instead of sending the matter to committee as new business, let it come to a board vote."
- "A leader told me, 'I don't understand why we must jump through so many hoops to get something done here. In my office, we just go ahead and do it. I don't understand the need for all this talking at committee meetings.' I replied, 'Things are different in a church.'"

Hold it off with your own Default Response:

- "Bring new business to the board only after proper committee and executive committee review and recommendations."
- "I respect that in your line of work, as a physician, you make many decisions yourself and quickly. But we work differently here. We should have a full discussion and seek consensus."
- "I don't see a committee review as 'a waste of time.' Their involvement will help them explain this change to the congregation. We need their support."
- "I recognize that you feel strongly about this issue. My concern is that others look at the matter differently. The committee is the place where we can talk through the differences."

Railroading is a strategy for avoiding opposition.

> "I understand that the committee voted as it did. But I wasn't invited to the meeting. I didn't even know about it. That is unacceptable to me. As the clergy, I need to be invited to a meeting where a matter of the pulpit was under discussion."

As mentioned in the preface, my interim instructor, Rev. Vicki Hall said, "God has special love for these people."

Pastor to the Body of the Congregation

"Someone Is Unhappy"

Many congregations harbor an unspoken assumption that everybody must be happy, and when someone gets upset, we must give them what they want, immediately, to restore their happiness (as described in Systems Theory, return the system to Equilibrium). "The customer," or congregant, "is always right," even when they are wrong, especially when that that customer is a significant donor, longtime member, or a leader. Responding to Someone Is Unhappy can consume a great deal of time and come at the expense of the congregation and the clergy.

In a world where pleasing everyone is impossible, it is far better to politely ask upset individuals to make peace with themselves and others and come together in peace on behalf of the greater good of the congregation. Our congregations operate at their best by clarifying the difference between having one's say, which is foundational, and getting one's way, which is conditional. Unfortunately, the task of ensuring universal happiness often falls to the clergy, who often feel responsible to address the concerns.

The best responses recognize the upset without agreeing to the substance:

- "I wish we could please everyone."
- "I don't like that either, but I am prepared to live with it."
- "What can we do to address the issue without compromising on our responsibility (or integrity)?"
- "A healthy congregation relies on members making their peace with things that bother them, for the sake of the greater good."

Stonewalling

Stonewalling creates a roadblock as a fait accompli. It is a preemptive action that shuts down contrarian conversation or behavior with a "yes, but . . . " Stonewalling is in:

"Rabbi, you are not here long enough to make this change."

An equally aggressive response would be:

"How long would I have to be here to open a discussion?"

Stonewalling is in:

"The temple would blow up if you raised that point."

And a response of equal emotional weight would be asking:

"How would that happen?"

Taking Disappearance of a Symptom for a Cure

Taking Disappearance of a Symptom for a Cure is a convenient way to avoid addressing a problem. For instance, the staff continues to suffer from an ongoing building issue (broken office air conditioner) or a personnel matter (grumpy and uncooperative custodian). Repeated complaints resulted in promises but no action. The staff eventually realize that they must deal with the problem for the foreseeable future (until fall brings cooler weather or the custodian retires). The leaders, who are in the building much less frequently than the staff, and do not encounter these issues, note that the complaining has stopped and incorrectly assume the issue has been resolved. When an executive committee member remarks, "I guess the problem has been addressed, since we haven't heard anything in a while," the minister replies, "The problem has not gone away. People are still unhappy but stopped complaining because they think that nothing will be done."

Other responses:

- "I was asked, 'Have things gotten better?' I replied, 'No, and I still feel the same way. But I don't like to nag.'"
- "I am on record. What I said still stands. Nothing changed, but there is nothing to be gained from harping on dissatisfaction."

Here, an interim succeeded in reducing an emeritus's intrusiveness, but the change could not be guaranteed to be sustained into the tenure of the incoming clergy:

> "When the congregational leader asked, 'The emeritus has been less involved lately, hasn't he?,' I said, 'He has been, but that could be because of how I treat him. When the successor comes, he may revert to his old ways.'"

This concludes our fusion of Empowerment and Systems Theory. Now we turn to the inevitable Transition and Farewell.

13

The Skills of Supporting Transition and Saying Goodbye

TRANSITION IS ABOUT THE congregation, Saying Goodbye is about you, and both blend as a tenure ends. Emotions turn to personal relationships that are closing and to new relationships and experiences that are about to begin. Feelings can be strong or subdued and can include denial, anger, relief, happiness, and sadness. There may be moving apart without speaking about it, or a Sense of Urgency may rise to spur unfinished business to completion in the remaining time.

Interims often hear, "It must be hard to leave a congregation at the end of each year. How do you deal with all those goodbyes?" It is hard when I-Thou turns to I-It. We work closely with the staff and leaders and have built strong working and personal relationships. Depending on the denomination, we are asked to stay away from the congregation for a year or more, so when we say goodbye to someone who is sick or dying, those farewell words are final.

Many interims seek distraction in the curiosity and excitement of starting again, which makes it easier to leave. As time passes, an interim will wonder about how some people they left behind are progressing, all the while knowing that the "primary client" is their clergy successor.

> "The exalted melancholy of our fate."[1]

Whether your departure follows your decision or theirs, whether you feel relief or happiness, the final months, weeks, and days of a tenure can be the hardest. People may see you as a "lame duck," hobbling along and oblivious until the final hour. After all, many in the congregation act that way when they leave a job. Call it a "Non-Anxious Non-Presence." You may feel left out when the leaders and your successor meet without you to become acquainted and plan. Those saddened by your departure, or unsure what to make of your successor, will try to put on a good face, but you see through it. Some will be angry at you or assume you have lost interest in them and let go of you early. It will be tempting to pull back.

Regardless of the circumstances and feelings, the final days are an opportunity to make an important difference by supporting the transition. Partnering and communicating with a successor and sustaining a Sense of Urgency and Holding to Task through your final days is the best way to stay relevant. Follow your successor's direction in setting a transition agenda. Above all, this a time to recognize accomplishments, and to identify and point out unaddressed goals.

> "A person does not pass from the moment of
> Supreme Meeting, the same being as they entered it
> ... something happens."[2]

---

1. Buber, *I and Thou*, 30.
2. Buber, *I and Thou*, 104.

Supporting Transition and Saying Goodbye

ATTEND TO YOURSELF DURING TRANSITION

Self-care is the first order of business. Review your tenure by asking:

- How have I changed?
- What am I most proud of?
- Where did I fall short?
- Was I mistreated?
- Did I mistreat or disappoint others?
- What is my next step?
- What kind of farewell do I want, and what are they planning?
- What am I:
  » Glad about?
  » Sad about?
  » Angry about?

We all fall short. Some of us are overly hard on ourselves, thinking, "If I worked harder, took more chances, or was more assertive, I would have been more effective." At the same time, we likely underestimate our impact. A good approach turns unfinished work into an agenda for the future.

ATTEND TO THE CONGREGATION DURING TRANSITION

The enhanced emotions of a transition create an opportunity to advance initiatives that were abandoned, neglected, or yet to be introduced. Embrace the anxious energy by creating a Sense of Urgency around a proposed change by simply saying:

- "Don't leave your next minister to deal with this problem."
- "Let's get this in place before I go for good."
- "Let's spare your next rabbi this headache."

Exit conversations resemble those you had upon entering. Again, follow your curiosity, Lead with Strengths, celebrate accomplishments, share the credit, and identify what is still needed. Be honest about what failed or what arouses disappointment.

While individual meetings continue to be the gold standard, group reflections with leaders and staff are also appropriate here. Go from general to specific and from specific to general. You can ask:

- What did you learn?
- You say it was a great year. What made it so?
- You say there were failures. What should I say to your next rabbi about that?
- What will you do differently?
- What do you hope stays the same?
- Was there a moment that stands out for you?

It can be hard to accept a compliment or hear that we meant something to someone else. Compliments may come across as exaggerated praise and unearned accolades. It is tempting to turn the conversation away from oneself, but stay on topic with grace.

During the Transition and Farewell Periods

Backsliding and Trying the Ending on for Size

People call Backsliding regression. One of my social work supervisors, Carl Carter, taught me that "when you get to the end, you go back to the beginning." Carl was not Jewish, but Jews do that on the holiday of Simhat Torah, when we traditionally read the final verses of Deuteronomy and immediately turn to read the opening words of Genesis, in a fusion of ending and beginning.

Both the clergy and the congregation may Backslide. On the other hand, you may see folks Try the Ending on for Size[3] by excit-

---

3. Shulman, *Skills of Helping Individuals*, 629.

edly pursuing new responsibilities or a new direction. Trying the Ending on for Size may include or exclude you. Take satisfaction from their show of readiness for their next chapter when they test out what they learned from you. If you are going to a new congregation, you are also likely Trying the Ending on for Size by becoming acquainted with the people there.

Doorknob Comments

Doorknob Comments[4] happen at departure, often within weeks or days. A Doorknob Comment comes in a rarely shared story of a stigmatizing personal experience. One congregant said to a departing clergy,

> "'I had to have an abortion twenty-five years ago, and I still think about it. I know I needed to do it, and I am glad I did, but I still think about it. Please keep this a secret. My husband is the only other person to know. Is that normal?' 'Yes, it is common,' said the minister who made a referral for consultation."

Or it could be something current:

> "A leader confided that he and his wife, who he is with all the time at the temple, have a 'horrible' marriage and that he is back to having an affair. I was surprised by what he said about the marriage, but I had nothing to say about the affair. It was beyond me."

The last-minute disclosure reflects respect for you and the fear that you will judge them negatively. If you react negatively, you will be gone, minimizing their hurt. If you show respect, you will be remembered fondly. The Doorknob Comment happens at the very end because the emotions over your departure grow so strong that they overcome the earlier hesitation over disclosure. It may be a plea for help that will carry on past your departure, with the hope that you will leave feeling sorry for them or that you will remain in their lives. Or it may be accompanied by the hope

---

4. Shulman, *Skills of Helping Individuals*, 235–36, 525–26.

that you will take this secret with you, and they do not have to be reminded of it each time they see you because they will not be seeing you anymore.

Farewell Party Effect

The Farewell Party Effect[5] is in unsuccessful attempts to cover up the sadness of ending with fun. It is that "goodbye lunch" marked by forced conversation over "your next chapter" and uncomfortable laughter that is supposed to wallpaper over grief, sadness, relief, and/or delight.

Explain Post-Tenure Boundaries

Be clear on the conditions of the ending, whether they are total or partial, permanent, or time-limited. These boundaries vary by denomination and may include:

- No contact with anyone for at least a year, except for the successor and any staff bound by a code of ethics
- No social engagements with former congregants
- No advice on congregational matters
- No pastoral contact
- Asking a leader for a reference is fine but only after informing the successor

These Boundaries often need to be explained to our congregants. People consider you a friend and do not immediately realize that this is a professional relationship. Pointing to denominational rules is futile for those who wonder why such rules should matter to a personal, private friendship. Dropping hints early avoids the shock of last-minute disclosures.

> "It is just like a psychotherapist when a relationship ends. It is just one year. I know it is hard. It is hard for me. But

---

5. Shulman, *Skills of Helping Individuals*, 629–30.

that next rabbi must go up there, and I cannot be in the picture."

As Buber said, this is "the exalted melancholy of our fate."[6] The end is holy, sad, and destined.

---

6. Buber, *I and Thou*, 30.

Afterword

THOSE LEADERS WHO APOLOGIZED after that upsetting first board meeting took responsibility for the health of their congregation, but I eventually came to see that it doesn't always work that way. In *A Failure of Nerve*, Rabbi Edwin Friedman maintains that many in authority in congregations and elsewhere find it hard to enter an emotionally charged situation and stand up for their beliefs and actions.

> "A board member with a reputation for being 'difficult' was not renewed for a second term, but no one ever told him. He found out by looking at the program at the congregational meeting. He was shocked. I was told that the leaders 'forgot' to tell him. It looked to me like they just avoided an uncomfortable situation."

One interim rabbi writes,

> "Shortly after I arrived as the congregation's interim, the youth advisor threatened to quit over her salary. She was getting mixed reviews to begin with, so I asked the leaders to let her go and assured them that the congregation would be better for it. Instead of listening to me, they gave in to her demands and explained that, with my predecessor's sudden departure and an interim, the congregation would become even more unsettled by yet another staff change. My heart sank. I should have told them to hold firm and that we would make things right. The year turned out poorly for the teens."

Our places of worship are a sanctuary, a refuge from the pressures and conflicts that consume communities, the media, the nation, and the world. Our faithful seek a congregation as a safe space that embodies that unachievable ideal of the twenty-third psalm's abundantly overflowing cup on a set table beside still waters. Who joins a congregation to jump into a board fight over some operational item? I admire those leaders who hold a high vision, cling to it, look beyond the expedient, and do what is right.

Effective and fulfilled clergy lead with strengths, delegate authority, and act with integrity. Beyond that, I wish I could magically empower all of us, clergy and leaders alike, to stand up for our beliefs with integrity, respect, and warmth, out of a recognition that God has special love for each person and that we are agents of bringing that divine presence into their lives.

APPENDIX A

Case Studies

A PROBLEM WITH ORGANIZED RELIGION

"I was meeting a prospective member on Zoom to discuss enrolling her kids. 'There's just one challenge,' she said. 'My husband has a problem with organized religion.'"

What do you say?
Some clergy would pick an argument.

- "When you weigh the pluses and minuses of religion, you see that the world is better with us."
- "Clergy, like everyone, make mistakes. But don't judge all religious people by a few bad errors."
- "Religion is perfect. People aren't, so don't blame religion for the bad things people do."

Aggressive/defensive responses include:

- "What do you mean by 'organized religion'"?
- "Lots of people attack religion by saying religion causes war. But war happens for many reasons, such as money, oil, or water. You're not going to take a vow of poverty, stop driving your car, or stop drinking water. Why pick on religion?

- "Karl Marx called religion the 'opiate of the masses.' Others call us a crutch for the weak. The reality is that very smart and very strong people are religious."

Other clergy take a more pastoral approach. Instead of making statements, they ask:

- "How long has this disagreement been going on?"
- "When did you first notice it?"
- "What do your children say?"
- "Why is this an issue right now? What's happening?"

Some clergy will request a more extended conversation with the couple to explore:

- "Are your parents pressuring you?"
- "What's your husband's religious upbringing?"
- "Where else do you two disagree?"
- "What do you think when you hear 'organized religion?'"

Here is the response and what happened.

> "Instead of disputing his position or acting like a marriage counselor, I said, 'I am glad you raised this with me because I have a problem with organized religion, too.' She looked surprised. I offered to speak with them both. We chatted a little more and then said goodbye. A week later, I learned that the family joined the congregation."

Why Did This Work?

The clergy countered expectation. You don't expect clergy to have problems with "organized religion," but many do. The problems range from long hours and low wages to disagreement with board decisions and conflict with denominational policies. Yet, religious outsiders are surprised to learn that clergy, the embodiment of "organized religion," have their own problems with "organized religion," whatever "organized religion" really is.

The minister's response had an unexpected and powerful emotional impact. It turned the negative energy in a productive direction—they joined! Where she expected an argument, the minister agreed with the husband. The minister reflected:

> "It worked like magic. It is counterintuitive that I am here. It was the most honest thing I could say. What is more, the Hebrew Bible has plenty of 'problems' with its characters. Just look at Adam and Eve in the garden of Eden."

This is an Empowerment Approach:

> "I respect the husband's opinion, and I wanted to make sure that I said something that recognizes that, even though I act differently than he does. I am not going to argue with him, ask him to explain himself to me, or try to 'save' him from himself, unless he wants that. Even if he wants nothing to do with me, I will ask him to respect my position, even as I respect his. Bottom line, he should decide the course of his life, not me."

The response restructured the Triangle:

> "By agreeing with him, I put her in the Lone Corner, even as I said I appreciated her contacting me."

The conversation began with the minister and the woman in alliance and the husband in the triangle's Lone Corner. The minister's response rebuilt the Triangle without being defensive or attacking.

> "I didn't want to appear threatened, spineless, or angry. I don't need to disprove his statement to be who I am. The reality is that most people in the world are not of my faith, and I do not need them to be."

As an example of the Non-Anxious Presence, the minister responded faithfully without getting emotionally overinvolved or taking responsibility for fixing the situation.

Appendix A

> "She basically was asking me to fix this for her. Instead, I let the problem stand and showed I cared, all at the same time. I haven't met him yet, so I assume he continues to have his 'problem.' I am open to discussing it, if he wishes. But I am not here to decide for them. I am willing to help them reach a decision that is right for them."

Clergy are not experts in mediating or in ironing out disagreements. Our expertise is in listening, supporting, advising, and offering hope and encouragement from the sidelines.

The response did not seek to explore the past. It led to forward conversation and action.

> "I'll talk about family history if they want, but my priority is supporting them in the present. And, if we do look at the past, we are not going to blame or punish anyone. Instead, we will set the stage for how they want to advance."

It was a Parsimonious response.

> "I wanted to be as simple as possible. Time is my only asset, and I am responsible for myself and the congregation to make efficient use of my time. You could see I addressed the problem with just one sentence."

They spoke as "I and Thou."

> "She came away with a clear understanding of where I stand, just as I came away having learned about their family. To be sure, any pastoral conversation is imbalanced, just like I-It. As a pastoral counselor, I see into someone else's life in a way that they do not see into mine. But, for that moment of communication about 'organized religion,' it felt like we experienced each other's presence as I-Thou."

CLOSING PRESCHOOL

> "It came up during my first interview to be their interim. Enrollment dropped from a high of ninety to a projected

dozen. The deficit was draining the budget, and there was a longstanding desire to sunset the program. This was just one of several major challenges in this declining congregation."

It is appropriate to take such a major step during interim tenure. However, the leaders focused on finances and unfortunately ignored the human impact on the families and staff.

"One officer told me that this is just a matter of money. 'This is adding to our deficit. That seals the argument.'"

It was a mistake to focus on the money and ignore the people.

"We assumed that we were giving parents and teachers enough time to get settled for the coming fall. We took that for granted without talking to anybody.

"The closure proposal went right to the executive committee, without consulting any other congregational body. It sailed through and then on to the board, which, after a brief discussion, voted for closure."

It took on the optics of a railroading.

"No one, not even me, anticipated the strong negative reaction from the families and the preschool staff. The preschool director understood, but she was on the edge of retiring anyway. But none of the families or other staff knew about the leadership discussion. The morning after the vote, the president and I met with the teachers, and we sent a letter to the congregation. The reaction was terrible. The teachers were a solid team and came out of the meeting heartbroken. The parents were shocked and angry about being forced to suddenly scramble for a place to send their kids. We heard things like 'Why didn't you warn us? You just rammed this through the board without telling us! Don't you care about us!? You are throwing us out into the cold!'"

The reality is that there is no good way to close a major program like this, regardless of when or which stakeholders are consulted.

Appendix A

Anyone negatively impacted will be left with nothing good to say about the decision or how the decision was reached.

> "When parents and teachers complained to me, I told them that I misjudged. I thought that people would reject such a small school. I thought everyone would agree that a school for ten kids is no school, but I was wrong. This was precisely the kind of school they wanted."

A group organized to "save" the preschool.

> "The arguments for reversing the decision were entirely emotional and not based on reality. We heard, 'I am convinced people are out there. If we keep it open, they will surely come!' or 'All three of our kids went through the preschool. How can we let it close?' Meanwhile, people paid no attention to the other preschools in the area that had closed in recent years, all for the same reason."

The leaders called a congregational meeting, which finally sealed the matter.

> "Some of the parents showed up but most didn't. The meeting got nasty. 'We're the outcasts of the congregation,' shouted one father. But nothing came of the meeting."

As for the outcome:

> "People were resigned to the decision. Only two of the ten families were our members. One of the two families quit, despite our efforts to keep them. The other family remained, and, to my surprise, the family stayed active. One of the parents even went into leadership."

As the Non-Anxious Presence, the Clergy:

- As an interim, spared the successor from facing a difficult situation and the resulting political repercussions
- Was an inadequate Presence to the families and staff

Case Studies

THE BLACK LIVES MATTER FLAG

> "One of our officers tipped me off about an upcoming complaint about a Black Lives Matter Flag on the pulpit. I noticed it the first time I came here. My predecessor put it up after talking to just a couple leaders. There never was a vote or anything. I decided though that if a member wants to see it come down, the request had to go to the board and that I would support retaining the flag."

While the pulpit is often seen as entirely the responsibility of the clergy, certain decisions are shared with the leaders. Unlike liturgy or preaching overseen and directed by the clergy, with input from the leaders and members, decisions about the physical adornments and how they are placed is a shared responsibility.

> "The call came a few days later, and she jumped right into it. 'I'm welcoming of all people, Reverend. That is not the problem. My concern is that the Black Lives Matter Flag is right next to the American flag, which means the church is elevating inclusion of Black people with love of country. I can't accept that.'"

The clergy stayed on the "prepared script":

> "I said, 'As you know, I wasn't part of those earlier conversations because I wasn't here, but I guess we can agree that putting a Black Lives Matter flag alongside the others was intended to send just that message.' I added that taking it down would require a board vote. I also wanted her to know where I stood, so that if the request came to the board, I would speak to retain the flag She said nothing."

The clergy went deeper.

> "I said, 'If it was up to me, I would put it out on the front entrance, where it would get more visibility. People passing by could see it.' She grunted."

The rabbi was playful, even baiting, a risky strategy which appeared to increase the caller's irritation.

Appendix A

> "She asked me what I would say to proposals about other flags on the pulpit. Would I object to a pulpit full of them? 'What would the board say to that?' I said, 'I suppose the board would consider each flag individually and decide what to do about each one.' I sensed she wanted me to answer yes or no, but I don't need to be specific about a hypothetical question."

An imaginary scenario gets an imaginary response.

The clergy held to the Pivot from Content to Process.

> "She continued. 'What about a pride flag? What would you say about that?' I said that the board would consider this request like any of the others, and if the supporter called me, 'I would hear them out, just as I am listening to you, and come to my conclusion, depending on what I heard and would think at the time.' She then said, 'Let me ask you about immigration. What do you think of these recent deportations?' I said that I had to get off the phone and would be willing to talk later in the week. She never reached out again."

As the Non-Anxious Presence, the clergy:

- Showed that they were listening without agreeing
- Pivoted from Content to Process by turning a conversation about what the flag symbolizes to who decides on the placement
- Established leeway to accept or reject further statements
- Described without getting defensive
- Did not personally endorse or reject the association of Black Lives Matter and patriotism, yet offered an implicit endorsement by officiating under it each week
- Identified a Boundary by affirming the board's authority
- Did not mention faith teachings
- Reset a Triangle that put the congregant in the Lone Corner in place of the clergy.

Case Studies

FIRING THE OFFICE MANAGER

During an interim tenure, a congregation has an opportunity to address longstanding issues such as the need to dismiss an underperforming staffer. It is for the interim, as the clergy in charge, to bear the brunt of the anger and spare the successor the burden.

> "My predecessor said the office manager should have been let go years earlier, and I could see why, even before I started. I also heard that the congregation was receiving substantial grant money, and the manager knew all the ins and outs of the application and renewal process, and she had longstanding relationships with the funding office."

We hear that all the time. "He is the only one who can do the job" or "we would be lost without her." These Default Responses reflect a reluctance to deal with a confrontation. It is more expedient to let the problem just be. Yet the responsibility for termination rests with the leaders, not the clergy.

> "The manager had terrible anger flashes, bolted out of the office when confronted, and stayed away for the rest of the day. I told the manager that these are serious issues and got a blank response."

This was a first-level, parsimonious response. There were no threats. It was a simple statement and included an opportunity for the manager to respond at that moment or later.

> "This was during Covid, and the manager refused to properly mask, despite my repeated requests. I decided that this insubordination deserved a second-level warning, so I emailed the manager, open copy to the senior leaders, offering a summary of what happened and a request to mask going forward. She replied immediately, with snark: 'A person has to eat and drink,' as if expressing self-congratulations for outsmarting the minister. I decided to let the matter rest for the time."
>
> "Shortly after, in a congregation that required board approval for all hirings, the manager and house

Appendix A

committee chair, without consulting anyone, collaborated to hire the manager's adult child as a custodian. I let that go. After a few days, the manager sent the senior leaders and me a copy of a negative background report, instructing us, 'Do not take the police record seriously. It was about a purely domestic thing and has nothing to do with the church.' I wrote back immediately, one sentence, copy to all: 'Tell him he's fired.' She responded immediately, 'Some minister you are. Here he is with a domestic problem and, instead of offering him counsel, you fire him.' I wrote back, copy to everyone, 'I counsel people before I fire them, not after. I can refer him to another minister if he wants pastoral counsel.'"

The minister presumed the leaders would agree and they did. A few weeks later:

"The house committee chair came in to see me. He offered to rehire the manager's son and pay his salary out of his own pocket. I was in no mood to compromise. I said that the negative report was a serious matter and that, regardless of who paid, the church could not have him on the payroll. 'How about outside the building?' and I said, 'not on the property.' He yelled, 'Reverend, this church will die because of you!' and he bolted out."

The minister should have sent this request to the leaders, accompanied by a strong recommendation that the offer be declined. The minister also did not respond to the angry comment that the "church will die."

"We were not done with the office manager. Our preschool director, who had enough from the manager long before I got there, called to say that, when one of the teachers asked the manager about a snack order, the manager responded, 'F@@# you and your food.' I said that I would file a grievance with the board on behalf of the teacher, but the teacher did not want to get involved. I felt I needed a name and a partner in the complaint, but I had to drop it. It was frustrating. Finally, when a large donor complained about rude treatment, the leaders faced the issue and dismissed the manager."

As the NAP, the clergy:

- Properly placed responsibility for the manager's dismissal, and the consequences for not dismissing, on the leaders
- Confronted the manager with a summary of concerns without blaming, threatening, or pulling rank
- Withheld response to the manager's response to the written request for masking
- Asked the preschool director to submit a grievance and offered to bring it to the leaders
- Engaged with the house chair and held firm but did not challenge the overreaction
- Overstepped by writing that the custodian was fired

APPENDIX B

Sample Work Plans

SPRING CONCERT

Task	Responsibility	Deadline	Date Completed
Appoint event chair (EC)	President, Clergy, Program VP		
Inform (obtain approval) board/committee	EC and VP		
Select date	Music director (MD), clergy, office manager (OM)		
Build committee	EC		
Book professional choir	MD		
Select theme	EC, MD, clergy		
Develop publicity plan	EC, VP, OM		
Develop fundraising plan	VP, EC, finance VP, and MD		
Design and print tickets	OM		
Invite guest soloists	MD		
Hire musicians	MD		
Sell tickets	OM		
Sign up ushers and ticket-takers	OM		
Provide OM with program text	EC, MD		
Design and print programs	MD		
Plan menu and order food	EC, OM		

APPENDIX B

ADULT STUDY RETREAT

Task	Responsibility	Deadline	Date Completed
Appoint event chair (EC)	President, clergy, VP		
Inform (obtain approval) board/committee	EC, VP		
Determine venue	EC, VP, clergy		
Set date	EC, clergy, office manager (OM)		
Build committee	EC		
Determine theme	EC, clergy		
Plan study program	Clergy, EC		
Distribute "save the date"	EC, OM		
Plan publicity schedule	EC, OM		
Plan program schedule	EC, clergy		
Open registration	OM		
Order supplies	OM		
Plan menu and order food	EC, OM		
Provide OM with study materials to duplicate	Clergy		
Distribute memo to participants	EC		

SAMPLE WORK PLANS

RESTORED CONFIRMATION PROGRAM

Task	Responsibility	Deadline	Date Completed
Inform religious school committee and ED VP	Clergy, education director (ED)		
Initial planning	Clergy and ED		
Meet with parent stakeholders	Clergy and ED		
Set schedule, curriculum	ED and clergy		
Meet with teens and parents	Clergy and ED		
Open registration	ED and OM		
Order supplies	OM and ED		
Distribute "welcome letter"	OM		
Send reminder before first session	OM		

APPENDIX C

The Skills of Media Interviewing

A REQUEST FOR A media interview—podcast, radio, TV—provides a wonderful yet challenging opportunity for promoting a congregation. This section describes basic media protocols such as how to decide whether to accept an interview request, how to graciously decline, and, when accepting an interview, how to stay on point and avoid being quoted out of context.

Most reporters are honest, straightforward, and accurate. Like anyone else who works, they face constant and firm deadlines, which can make them appear to be disinterested or in a hurry. Regardless, clergy should weigh each media request individually.

DECIDE WHETHER TO ACCEPT OR DECLINE AN INTERVIEW REQUEST

There is nothing wrong with declining a press call. Everyone does. You should decline when a reporter says:

- "We'd like to run a story on why you are leaving your congregation" when the details are personal and private.
- "Can you comment on the charges of antisemitism at the local college?" when you are not familiar with the situation and, with two funerals that week, do not want to devote the time to researching this matter.

- "One of your members was arrested for fraud. What are people in the congregation saying?" This is a pastoral matter, and you do not want to be quoted in the press.

Most interview requests are not some kind of trap, but clergy need to be careful. To help with your decision, search the web for the reporter's work. You may find something positive and reassuring or something else that makes you think you will not be covered fairly. Note that TV, podcasts, and radio talk show interviews are intended to make the host look good, even at your expense. Do not expect to overtalk your host or prove your host wrong. What is more, you should be able to trust your host not to cut you off on a live show or edit you down on a recording. Decline these invitations.

You should also consider declining if:

- You got hate mail after a previous interview, and you don't want more
- A clergy colleague had a terrible experience with this reporter
- The last time you dealt with this reporter, they tried to trap you
- You are concerned about a news report that would reflect negatively on the congregation or yourself

There is no need to decide about an interview on the spot. To help with the decision, ask the reporter:

- "When is your deadline?"
- "What is your angle?"
- "Who else are you talking to?"
- "What will you want to ask me?"

Avoid declining with "no comment." It looks like you are trying to hide something. Better to say:

- "I am too busy to talk."

Appendix C

- "I am part of a community coalition, and I am not authorized to speak for them."
- "I'm busy with other things right now and can't meet your deadline."
- "I need to organize my thoughts."
- "I am preparing to officiate at two funerals tomorrow."
- "I must go see someone in the hospital now."
- "I need to get approval from the leaders." (In the very least, you should let them know that the press called, regardless of what you decide.)
- "I know you want to talk about this now. But it is not a good time for me. Please call me next week."

HOLD TO FOCUS WHEN THE MEDIA CALLS

Once you accept an interview, then decide what you want to say. By way of background, there is a world of difference between talking to a reporter and talking to a friend. When speaking with the media, think of Martin Buber: we have I-Thou with friends, but it is all I-It with the press. Hold to Focus. Instead of providing rambling or spontaneous responses to reporters, prepare what you want to say and stick to your plan. Again, reporters are just doing their job. But, as has been said in the communications field, "You are not there to answer a reporter's questions. Reporters are there to report what you say." Thus, it is critical to distinguish between the careful listening and empathic responses of a pastoral conversation and a press interview, where it is important to stick to a prepared message. You must control what you say.

How many times have we heard "that reporter quoted me out of context. I was talking about something else, but they took what I said to make a point I didn't want to make?" There is no such thing as being "quoted out of context." You said it, and they wrote it down. Expect to be asked questions you do not want to answer. Keep to your prepared remarks throughout, regardless of the questions.

If you decide to accept an interview:

- Prepare your response. Stay on point, and you will not be "quoted out of context"
- Keep it simple
- Speak in a positive voice
- Say, "I don't know" when that is true

STAY ON POINT

There's an art to staying on point without looking like you are avoiding tough questions or being dishonest or cagey. When asked a question you are unprepared to answer, or do not want to discuss, change the topic and be honest about it. Touch on the question and then redirect the conversation to what you wanted to discuss your topic. "Pivot" to your prepared remarks by saying:

- "I hear your question" and then go back to your point
- "I think people really want to know what I just said a moment ago, that . . ."
- "I understand your question, but I think it is more important to remember . . ."
- Repeat yourself by saying, "Again . . ." or "Let me repeat myself . . ."

You can also:

- Go smaller: "I hear your question. I am here to focus on one very small but critical point"
- Go bigger: "Yes, that's important. Let's take a step back and consider the larger problem"
- Go to something else: "I know you want to know about that. I am here to talk about another thing." Or "I respect your concern, but we need to speak about a different matter."

Appendix C

Acknowledge the unwanted question, and then return to what you want to say.

You may be asked for a closing comment. Take advantage of that question to go back and repeat your key point.

- "As I said, we need to realize..."
- "Let's not forget that the most important thing is..."
- "I need to underscore that..."

Finally, *never* go "off the record." It has been said in media circles, "Fiends keep secrets. Reporters report them." Despite any promise, you may be quoted anonymously or referenced in a way that can get back to you.

Bibliography and for Further Reading

Bendroth, Norman B. *Interim Ministry in Action: A Handbook for Churches in Transition*. Lanham, MD: Rowman & Littlefield, 2018.
Bolsinger, Tod. *Tempered Resilience Study Guide: 8 Sessions on Becoming an Adaptive Leader*. Downers Grove, IL: InterVarsity, 2020.
Bowen, Murray. *Family Therapy in Clinical Practice*. Lanham, MD: Jason Aronson, 1993.
Bradshaw, Anita L. *Change and Conflict in Your Congregation: Even If You Hate Both*. Woodstock, VT: SkyLight Paths, 2015.
Braeger, George, and Stephen Holloway. *Changing Human Services Organizations: Politics and Practice*. New York: Free, 1978.
Bridges, William, and Susan Bridges. *Managing Transitions: Making the Most of Change*. Boston: Da Capo Lifelong, 2006.
Brown, Jenny, and Lauren Errington. *Bowen Family Systems Theory in Christian Ministry: Coping with Theory and Its Application Through a Biblical Lens*. Neutral Bay, Australia: Family Systems Practice & Institute, 2019.
Buber, Martin. *Daniel: Dialogues on Realization*. Syracuse, NY: Syracuse University Press, 2018.
———. *I and Thou*. Translated by Ronald Gregor Smith. New York: Scribner, 2000.
———. *On the Bible*. New York: Schocken, 1968.
———. *Tales of the Hasidim: Early Masters*. New York: Schocken, 1975.
———. *Tales of the Hasidim: Later Masters*. New York: Schocken, 1948.
Cooley, Terasa. *Transforming Conflict: The Blessing of Congregational Turmoil*. Lanham: MD: Alban, 2022.
Cox, David. "The Edwin Friedman Model of Family Systems Thinking." *Academic Leadership: The Online Journal* 4 (2006) Article 10. https://scholars.fhsu.edu/cgi/viewcontent.cgi?article=1115&context=alj.
Creech, R. Robert. *Family Systems and Congregational Life: A Map for Ministry*. Grand Rapids: Baker Academic, 2019.
Friedman, Edwin H. *A Failure of Nerve: Leadership in the Age of the Quick Fix*. New York: Seabury, 2007.

———. *From Generation to Generation: Family Process in Church and Synagogue.* New York: Guilford, 1985.

Friedman, Maurice. *Encounter on the Narrow Ridge: A Life of Martin Buber.* New York: Paragon, 1993.

Gilbert, Roberta M., and Greg Jacobs. *The Eight Concepts of Bowen Theory.* Minneapolis: Leading Systems, 2018.

Hepworth, Dean H., et al. *Direct Social Work Practice: Theory and Skills.* Boston: Cengage, 2013.

Kerr, Michael E., and Murray Bowen. *Family Evaluation.* New York: W. W. Norton, 1988.

Laufer, Nathan. *The Genesis of Leadership: What the Bible Teaches Us About Vision, Values, and Leading Change.* Woodstock, VT: Jewish Lights, 2006.

Leas, Speed. *Discover Your Management Style.* Herndon, VA: Alban, 1997.

———., and Paul Kittlaus. *Church Fights: Managing Conflict in the Local Church.* Philadelphia: Westminster, 1973.

Lederman, Esther. "Creating a Culture of Experimentation in Your Congregation." May 15, 2017. https://urj.org/blog/creating-culture-experimentation-your-congregation.

Parsons, George, and Speed B. Leas. *Understanding Your Congregation as a System: The Manual.* Herndon, VA: Alban, 1993.

Reeves, Ken. *The Whole Church: Congregational Leadership Guided by Systems Theory.* Lanham, MD: Rowman & Littlefield, 2009.

Rendle, Gilbert R. *Leading Change in the Congregation: Spiritual and Organizational Tools for Leaders.* Lanham, MD: Alban Institute, 1998.

———. *Quietly Courageous: Leading the Church in a Changing World.* Lanham, MD: Rowman & Littlefield, 2019.

Shitama, Jack. *Anxious Church for Anxious People.* Earleville, MD: Charis Works, 2018.

———. *If You Met My Family, You'd Understand: A Family Systems Primer.* Earleville, MD: Charis Works, 2020.

———., and Trinity McFadden. *Everyone Loves a Non-Anxious Presence: Calm Down, Grow Up, and Live Your Best Life.* Earleville, MD: Charis Works, 2023.

Shulman, Lawrence. *The Skills of Helping Individuals, Families, Groups, and Communities.* 8th ed. Boston: Cengage, 2020.

Steineke, Peter L. *How Your 21st-Century Church Family Works: Understanding Congregations as Emotional Systems.* Lanham, MD: Rowman & Littlefield, 2021.

Wesse, Carolyn, and J. Russell Crabtree. *The Elephant in the Boardroom: Speaking the Unspoken About Pastoral Transitions.* San Francisco: Josey-Bass, 2004.

Woods, Mary E., and Florence Hollis. *Casework: A Psychosocial Therapy.* 5th ed. Boston: McGraw-Hill, 2000.

www.ingramcontent.com/pod-product-compliance
Lightning Source LLC
Chambersburg PA
CBHW062039220426
43662CB00010B/1563